Railway Memories No. 29

THE BLYTH & TYNE
and associated colliery railways

Written and compiled by Stephen Chapman

BELLCODE BOOKS
Church View, Middle Street
Rudston, East Yorkshire YO25 4UF
email: bellcode4books@yahoo.co.uk

Copyright © 2016 Bellcode Books
ISBN 9781871233 31 5

All rights reserved. The contents of this book are the copyright of Bellcode Books and their contributors and may not be reproduced in any form or posted on any internet website without the prior written consent of the copyright holder.

Designed and edited by Stephen Chapman

Printed in the UK by the Amadeus Press, Cleckheaton, West Yorkshire.

ABOVE: The National Coal Board lines were as big a part of the railway scene in this part of Northumberland as British Railways. At Backworth, NCB Austerity 0-6-0ST No.48(Hunslet 2864 of 1943) shunts BR hopper wagons in the sidings near the crossing with the B1322 road on Friday 30th May 1975. *Adrian Booth*
FRONT COVER: In the Blyth and Tyne area, British Railways trains could be seen venturing along National Coal Board railways which were fully signalled accordingly. Its smokebox scorched by its labours, Blyth J27 0-6-0 No. 65879 passes Camperdown on the NCB line to Burradon with 21-ton hoppers from the BR line at Holywell Junction. *S.M. Watkins/Colour-Rail*
BACK COVER TOP: On the Burradon & Holywell wagonway, NCB Austerity 0-6-0ST No. 9(Robert Stephenson & Hawthorns 7097 of 1943) threads green pastures and willow herb whilst approaching Backworth with empties from Weetslade washery on Tuesday 12th August 1975. Backworth sent its coal to Weetslade for washing after its washer failed in summer 1974. The signal marks the start of the section to Holywell Junction where the wagonway joined the Blyth & Tyne. *Stephen Chapman*
BACK COVER BOTTOM: In Spring 2011 GB Railfreight hired in locomotives to cover a short-term motive power shortage. One of those so hired was Deltic No. 55022 *Royal Scots Grey* which was used to work the North Blyth-Lynemouth alumina trains. It is seen passing Freeman's Crossing with a loaded train to Lynemouth on 12th April 2011. *John Lewins*
FRONTISPIECE: A classic early 1950s railway scene at Percy Main, the southern end of the Blyth & Tyne where J27 0-6-0 No. 65809 is dealing with a train load of pit props. Behind it empty wagons are being shunted on the lines to Northumberland Dock in front of Engine Shed signal box. Left of the box is the coaling stage for Percy Main engine shed and left of that are lines to the Tyne Improvement Commission's extensive dock railway system. *Neville Stead collection*

The publisher's thanks are due to all those who have provided material for this edition of Railway Memories. Also to Adrian Booth, Ron Hollier and Neville Stead for their assistance. **Sources:** BR and LNER documents, working timetables, appendices, notices, press releases and publicity publications; Clinker's Register of Closed Lines and Stations; Durham Mining Museum; Industrial Railway Society; LNER List of Lines; The North Eastern Area, a paper for the LNER by C.B. Fawcett, B.Litt. Reader in Geography, Leeds University; North Eastern Express - the journal of the North Eastern Railway Association; Official Handbook of Stations 1956, The Railway Clearing House; The Ordnance Survey; Railnews; A Regional History of Railways, North East England, K. Hoole, David & Charles; Tyneside Tramroads of Northumberland, a paper by Charles E. Lee FRSA, M. Inst. T. etc, member of the council of the Newcomen Society; contempory editions of Modern Railways, Railway Magazine, The Railway Observer, Railway World and Trains Illustrated.
Important: Bellcode Books is not in a position to supply or locate copies of photographs reproduced in this book so please don't ask.

INTRODUCTION

Mention the Blyth & Tyne, and a rather unique, self-contained and independent railway comes to mind.

Although originating in the 1840s, the Blyth & Tyne was exceptional in not being a product of the Railway Mania. Instead, it was a combination of colliery lines with one purpose in mind - to carry coal to the Tyne for shipping.

From the very beginnings it has had a self-contained uniqueness about it which, although losing its independence as long ago as 1874, remains to this day.

Alongside the B&T was a network of colliery railways and wagonways which entwined themselves around it like vines on a pole, creating a network of utmost fascination until the major closures which began in 1960. The biggest of the colliery systems, the Hartley Main, ran to main line standards with signalling, brake vans, and tender engines, some of historic main line vintage.

The nature of these railways' and the B&T's location, somewhat off the beaten track, rendered them beyond the reach of many enthusiasts of the time except by means of the occasional railtour. Even so, there were those who managed to record on film the Blyth & Tyne, the colliery lines and their very special engines when they were still an everyday sight, leaving a legacy of wonderful pictures for us to enjoy in this edition of Railway Memories. And to them we pay tribute.

On 7th September 1964, British Railways began using the 24-hour clock in its working timetables so we use am/pm up to that date and the 24-hour clock thereafter.

BR Sectional Appendix supplements are quoted herein as the date for various changes to signalling etc. It should be noted that the actual change may have taken place well before the supplement was issued.

Contents

Page 4	The Blyth & Tyne story
Page 24	Manors North-Monkseaton
Page 33	Backworth-Morpeth
Page 50	Bedlington-Newbiggin
Page 56	North and South Blyth
Page 83	Earsdon Junction-Percy Main
Page 92	The colliery railways

A vision of how things might have looked on the old Blyth & Tyne Railway. Hartley Main Coal Co. double framed 0-6-0 No. 3, seen at Percy Main in May 1935, is equipped with a genuine Blyth & Tyne tender, 60 years after the B&T ceased to exist as an independent concern. *Neville Stead collection*

The Blyth & Tyne story

The year 1649 was a defining moment in British history. The king of England had been executed and the country was a republic governed by Parliament. That same year, Newcastle merchant William Gray referred to the use of wagonways for carrying coal in his Chorographia - a survey of Newcastle-upon-Tyne. Events that would ultimately lead to the main line railways we have today - and the Blyth & Tyne in particular - were in motion.

On a local level, these horse-powered wooden wagonways - carrying coal from numerous small pits to the nearest stretch of navigable water from where it could be delivered to its consumers by boat - the best means of bulk transport then available - would evolve into an intense network of colliery lines that would remain in operation almost to the end of the 20th century. Some would be incorporated - by Parliament - into the Blyth & Tyne Railway, the spinal main public railway serving the east Northumberland coalfield.

To state when the first wagonway was established in Northumberland is a risky business that would almost certainly invite contradiction, but Gray noted that midlander Huntington Beaumont - generally credited with establishing Britain's first wagonway in Nottinghamshire in 1597 - had taken over failing coal pits at Bebside and Cowpen from Peter Delaval in 1605. Gray wrote that "Master Beaumont....brought many rare engines not known to these parts, as the art to bore with iron rodds to try the deepnesse and thicknesse of the coale; rare engines to draw water out of the pits; waggons with one horse to carry down coales from the pits to the staithes..." This latter reference is generally interpreted as meaning wagons on rails since more than one horse was required for a road cart which was then referred to as a waine. Beaumont's venture had failed by 1614 and "500 paces" of rails to the mouth of the River Blyth were noted as being removed from the ground. In 1609 Blyth was recorded as shipping 21,571 tons of coal, the first year for such a large amount, reflecting the likelihood of the wagonway coming into operation.

Another wooden wagonway was thought to be carrying coal from pits around Whitley to Cullercoats for use at the salt pans there, possibly from as early as 1621 until the 1730s when the pits had to be abandoned due to flooding. From around 1709 the Plessey Wagonway was carrying coal 5 1/2 miles from Plessey Hall Farm to Blyth. Despite being abandoned by 1812, sections are still clearly visible just north of Cramlington while its route through Blyth is marked by Plessey Road. Over the ensuing 200 years wagonways would come and go as the coal industry evolved with the early pits and their wagonways being superseded by new collieries and railways.

In 1820, the Bedlington Iron Company laid a two-mile wagonway to carry coal from a mine at Choppington to its furnaces in Bedlington. It was laid with rolled iron rails (instead of cast iron) which were the brainchild of John Birkenshaw, the company's chief agent. Over the next five years the Bedlington Iron Company would manufacture them in large quantities, not least for George Stephenson and the Stockton & Darlington Railway. Modern railway track started here, in Bedlington. It may be mentioned at this point that Bedlington has another claim to fame in railway history, the Great Western Railway locomotive engineer Sir Daniel Gooch was born there in 1816.

The Blyth & Tyne Railway itself came into being in a rather piecemeal fashion and several early colliery lines would be crucial in that process. By the late 18th century Northumberland coal was regularly being taken by wagonway to three principal harbours for shipping - Blyth, Seaton Sluice and North Shields(Howdon, Hay Hole and Whitehill Point) on the Tyne. A map produced by William Gibson, amongst other things lawyer and Newcastle town clerk, in 1788 shows a wagonway from High Flatworth to a staith at Hay Hole which by 1812 had extended to pits at Murton Main and Shiremoor. The Percy Main wagonway from Percy Main Colliery to a staith at Howdon is recorded as having opened in 1801. A wagonway from Avenue Head, near Hartley, was taking coal from small pits in the area to Seaton Sluice, and by 1811 another was in operation from new mines around Whitley to the Tyne.

By the mid-1820s the Seghill Colliery was making use of the recently-opened Cramlington and Backworth colliery wagonways to send its coal to the Tyne. Then in 1838 the Seaton Delaval Coal Company completed a short line from its newly sunk colliery to the Cramlington Coal Company's line at Mare Lane, along which it too would send its coal to the Tyne. Two years later the Seghill Colliery owners opened their own line to the Tyne via Percy Main. They called it the Seghill Railway and it would be an important constituent of the Blyth & Tyne. In August 1841 it went so far as to start a public passenger service using coaches that were rudimentary to say the least. From 1844 the service was operated on its behalf by the Newcastle & North Shields Railway.

With the use of steam in factories and on railways gathering momentum, the quality steam coal produced by Northumberland pits was in ever increasing demand. But for the pits further north, Blyth harbour was still the only outlet and it was too shallow for the bigger ships now coming into use - which put those coalowners without access to the deeper waters of the Tyne at a considerable disadvantage when it came to selling their coal. Thus, access to the Tyne became essential.

The first move towards this end came when Jobling & Partners, the lessees of Cowpen and Hartley collieries, proposed a line connecting their pits directly to the Tyne. Their intended route was to make use of the afore-

Bedlington, a key junction on the Blyth & Tyne, has a significant place in railway history. This view showing Jubilee 4-6-0 No. 45562 *Alberta* heading a railtour returning to Leeds on Saturday 10th June 1967 was taken from Furnace Way Sidings, whose name recalls the ironworks which created the first rolled iron rails. The Ashington Railtour is seen on the section of line first opened by the Bedlington Coal Company in 1850. *Neville Stead collection*

mentioned Whitley wagonway on its way to the harbour at Low Lights, Tynemouth. In the event, they took this route only as far as Dairy House where they joined the existing wagonway to Seaton Sluice. Instead, their "main line" - The Blyth & Tyne Junction Railway - continued west from Hartley until it joined the Seghill Railway. The Blyth-Seghill section opened for mineral traffic in 1846 and by the time a passenger service was introduced in 1847, the whole route from Blyth to Percy Main had been renamed the Blyth, Seghill & Percy Main Railway, and then the Blyth & Tyne Railway, although it was still basically a collaboration of individual colliery lines.

While Seaton Sluice declined as a coal port, Blyth did not and in 1849 the Blyth & Tyne opened the first timber staiths there. A year later, the Bedlington Coal Company opened its own line for both minerals and passengers to Newsham where it joined the B&T, so now Bedlington was plugged into the network. A further development came in 1851 when the line was rebuilt to cut through Prospect Hill which stood to the north of Percy Main. This eliminated gradients as steep as 1 in 25 and allowed locomotives to be used throughout instead of the time-consuming inclines which were previously needed to take the line over the hill. Over the following few years a connection was laid to the Newcastle & North Shields line, bridges reconstructed, track doubled, branches laid to various shipping berths and gradients through Prospect Hill further eased.

Up to this point the wagonways and colliery lines had used wayleave agreements in order to cross landowners' estates, paying the landowner according to the tonnage of coal carried. This proved very lucrative for the landowners but not for the early railways since landowners often charged such exorbitant rates that the lines were rendered uneconomic to the point that they went out of business. With numerous individual agreements it was also beurocratic - lucrative for lawyers but again, costly for the railways. This was where Parliament came in. An Act of Parliament gave the railways the right to cross land subject to various conditions being met and in 1852 an Act was passed officially consolidating the various lines which made up Blyth & Tyne Railway into one company, and replacing the wayleaves. The Blyth & Tyne as a public railway had come into being.

There was more to come, however. By 1857 the B&T had extended through to Morpeth, incorporating the Bedlington Coal Company line in the process. It had also bought the

This 1950s view of a Blyth-Monkseaton Railmotor entering Hartley station shows how the main Blyth & Tyne route turned sharply to the west and towards Seghill while the 1860 route to Monkseaton and Tynemouth continued straight on, thus necessitating a "V" shaped station. The driving trailer has "Hull" on the front. *The Late Rev. John Parker/Photos from the Fifties*

parallel Seaton Delaval company line, using it to double its main line. In return the B&T gave Seaton Delaval running powers over the 1.9 miles to Seghill Junction where its trains could join the Cramlington Railway.

At Morpeth the B&T set up its own terminus alongside the North Eastern Railway's station on the Newcastle-Berwick main line, a passenger service starting in April 1858. To create an outlet onto the B&T, the North Seaton Colliery had built its own line to Bedlington by 1859.

The following year, the B&T's original projected route was utilized when it opened the Avenue Line from Dairy House via Monkseaton to Tynemouth for both goods and passengers, the Tynemouth terminus being situated between the southern tip of Northumberland Park and the Master Mariner's Asylum, some way out of the town. By summer 1864 it had built a new curve at the Tynemouth end, first to a second, temporary, station closer to the town when the original terminus became a goods and coal depot, and then to the final terminus on a site adjacent to the present station.

In June 1864 the B&T opened another line which demonstrated that its intentions had gone way beyond just moving coal to the Tyne - and why its much bigger neighbour, the NER, would see it as a threat. This was its new line from Monkseaton to the heart of Newcastle at Picton Place(later renamed New Bridge Street) along with

a west-north curve from Backworth to Earsdon Junction where it crossed the Cramlington Railway on the level before joining the Blyth-Percy Main line. Picton Place station was designed by John Dobson, architect of Newcastle Central. Now the B&T could not only run passenger services from Blyth to Newcastle but also a commuter service from Tynemouth. Consequently, it saw no need for the Monkseaton-Hartley service and the Avenue Line closed to passengers along with the Earsdon Junction-Percy Main section. To make matters worse from the NER's point of view, the North British Railway had connected with the B&T at Morpeth, via a bridge over the NER's main line to a junction with the Bedlington branch at Shaw House where it also crossed the Netherton Colliery Wagonway. The North British could, if it wanted, run its trains via the B&T straight into the heart of Newcastle.

Further north, meanwhile, big new pits were opening near the Woodhorn Demesne(there was no Ashington before then,) most of them connected via their own lines to the NER main line, which for coal trains meant a roundabout run with two reversals in order to reach Blyth. For its part, the B&T opened a branch from West Sleekburn Junction, on the Bedlington-North Seaton Colliery line, to Cambois Colliery on the north bank of the Blyth in 1867. Then, in 1872, incorporating the North Seaton Colliery line, the

B&T completed the section from Bedlington to Ashington and Newbiggin. It now rivalled the NER for traffic from these new pits which it could move directly to Blyth or Percy Main.

The all-powerful NER could not allow this challenge to its monopoly and in 1874 it bought the B&T, and so the B&T's independent existence came to an end. And yet, while it was now just another section of the giant North Eastern Railway, its self-contained nature meant that the B&T would remain independent in character to the present day.

This was not the end of the B&T system's development, however. A major change came in July 1882 when the NER opened the coast line from Monkseaton, via new stations at Whitley Bay and Cullercoats, to Tynemouth where it connected with the Newcastle & North Shields to form a circular route from New Bridge Street to Newcastle Central. The B&T's inland route was closed and its Tynemouth terminus replaced by the present through station on the new line. The first terminus continued handling coal traffic until 1971, being connected to the new line by the 1864 curve. A stub was retained at the Monkseaton end for goods and carriage sidings.

At Morpeth, the B&T was connected to the East Coast main line and the NER station where new bay platforms were provided, the original B&T terminus also being converted into a goods depot. The North British was given running powers over the NER main line and the connection to Shaw House replaced by a junction with the main line. In 1888 a second line to Blyth was opened, from Newsham via Crofton Mill to serve new staiths. The year 1896 saw the opening of staiths at North Blyth, served by extending the Cambois branch. The curve from the Ashington line at Marcheys House to Winning Junction was also laid, enabling the direct movement of coal from Ashington to North Blyth staiths.

The first decade of the 20th century brought momentous changes which saw an important part of the Blyth & Tyne network take on a new role and finally give up its Blyth & Tyne identity in the name of technological progress. In a bold response to stiff competition from new electric trams, the NER electrified the whole of the North Tyne Loop from New Bridge Street to Monkseaton, Tynemouth and Newcastle Central on the 600 volts dc 3rd rail system during the course of 1904, transforming it into a modern suburban railway. The New Bridge Street-Benton section was completed in March and Benton-Monkseaton in June when the steam-operated Monkseaton-Hartley passenger service was reinstated. The trams had taken away 40 per cent of the railway's passengers but within 10 years of electrification the Loop was carrying more passengers than ever before. It was also encouraging growth in the coastal towns as seaside resorts and residential suburbs.

In conjunction with the electrification a new West-South curve was installed in 1903 from Benton station to the East

In the bay platforms created at Morpeth station to replace the separate Blyth & Tyne terminus after the NER take-over, G5 0-4-4T No. 67323 has charge of a special class B working on Saturday 14th July 1951. The engine has recently been transferred to South Blyth from Blaydon and still carries a 52C shedplate. *Neville Stead collection*

Coast main line at Benton Quarry Junction, mainly for the movement of empty trains between the car sheds at Walker Gate and New Bridge Street station. In July 1904 the South-East curve from Benton Quarry Junction to Benton East was opened, which would provide a direct route onto the B&T from Newcastle Central, especially for express electric services. In 1909 a new stretch of electrified line was opened between New Bridge Street and Manors South on the eastern approaches to Newcastle Central. This meant that all passenger trains on the Blyth & Tyne lines could reach Newcastle Central. New Bridge Street, the B&T's headquarters, was closed to passengers and converted into a goods station. A new through station was provided nearby at Manors North, where many Blyth and Newbiggin services continued to start and terminate to the end.

The Blyth & Tyne network was probably at its peak around this time though 1928 finally saw completion of the vast West Blyth staiths on the north bank of the river, construction having been held up by the first world war. Another victim of the Great War was an electrified branch which the NER was building to Seaton Sluice in the hope of encouraging residential development - for which Seaton Sluice was to be renamed the more appealing Collywell Bay. The branch was virtually complete with double track and station platforms in place when war broke out, but all track was then removed for re-use elsewhere and construction was not resumed when hostilities ended. In 1931 the NER's successor since the 1923 Grouping, the London & North Eastern Railway, abandoned the project entirely. The only traffic it had carried was a rail-mounted gun on temporary second hand track.

Another line was added to the network in 1939 when the LNER opened the two-mile branch from Murton Row to Rising Sun Colliery. It crossed over the Cramlington Railway at Murton Row by means of the bridge carrying the disused Seaton Burn wagonway. During the second world war, in 1940, the B&T was given an extra connection to the East Coast main line when a new Benton west-north curve was laid to provide an alternative route in the event of bombing around Heaton. In 1952 Bates Colliery, at Blyth, was connected to the B&T when British Railways took over and upgraded the former Cowpen Colliery Co. branch from Newsham to Isabella Pit where it connected with a newly-laid NCB line to Bates. For the previous 18 years since being opened, Bates had had no main line connection, the idea being that all its output would load straight into ships via internal railway and conveyors.

One other railway system worthy of mention in this section because it was connected directly to the Blyth & Tyne at Percy Main is the railway of the Tyne Improvement

In 1864 the Blyth & Tyne entered Newcastle at what became New Bridge Street. In 1904 the NER electrified it and turned it into a suburban railway of what was then cutting edge modernity, and in 1909 extended the line from New Bridge to Manors, enabling B&T passenger trains to reach Newcastle Central. In the 1950s, one of the North Tyneside articulated 3rd rail electric units built in the 1930s enters Newcastle Central with a service from the coast which may have travelled over the B&T section from Monkseaton. *Tom Greaves*

Commission(latterly the Port of Tyne Authority.) This was a complex system extending to 90 track miles, all contained in less than a square mile.

Established by Act of Parliament in 1850, the TIC wasted no time in setting about fulfiling its objectives of improving and developing the facilities for shipping on the Tyne. By 1857 it had completed the construction of the 55-acre Northumberland Dock which had the effect of enclosing the various coal staiths at Hay Hole within its tide-free basin, enabling ships to be loaded at any time. In 1884, immediately to the east, it opened the 23-acre Albert Edward Dock complete with its own enclosed coal staith, and around 400 acres of timber stacking grounds and associated railway sidings. An engine shed for the TIC railway's fleet of over a dozen shunting locomotives was situated south west of the dock basin, alongside the approaches to the coal staith. The two docks were separated by Whitehill Point, an area of land upon which stood a mass of railway, timber yards, timber storage sheds and warehouses, as well as coal staiths still reaching directly to the river.

Parts of the railway were operated to main line standards and fully signalled with its own signal boxes and a section of double track "main line." The boundary with the main line company was at TIC No.1 signal box between Percy Main and the approaches to Northumberland Dock. Full block signalling was a necessity as it carried main line passenger trains - such as The Norseman from London King's Cross - to Tyne Commission Quay for connection with Scandinavian ferries, but its main lifeblood was typical of any North East port: coal, timber, general cargo, grain and pit props. Added in 1928 to replace an earlier passenger jetty, Tyne Commission Quay consisted of two deep water berths each with its own rail terminus, one for Oslo ferries and one for Bergen ferries. These were set at right angles to each other with the Bergen berth on the riverside; a moveable platform across the track connected the two.

Colliery Railways

As if the story of how the public railway came to be isn't complicated enough, detailed analysis of the development of the many colliery railways and wagonways that crisscrossed Blyth & Tyne territory would demand an entire book of its own. In the 95 or so square miles between the East Coast main line and the sea, and the rivers Tyne and Lyne, there were an estimated 45 collieries served by a railway of some sort and many were interconnected by these mineral lines and wagonways.

The 20th century began with seven large mining concerns in the area, each owning several pits and its own railways. These were the the Ashington Coal Co., Backworth

Amid the vast expanse of timber stacking grounds, V1 2-6-2T No. 67645 passes T.I.C. No. 6 signal box with a boat train from the Tyne Commission Quay. The line on the right leads to the various coal staiths at Whitehill Point via No. 9 signal box - just visible on the far right - and a connection with the Backworth Railway situated on the embankment in the centre background. *Neville Stead collection*

Collieries Ltd., the Bedlington Coal Co., the Cowpen Coal Co., the Cramlington Coal Co., the Seaton Burn Coal Co. (owning Seaton Burn and Dinnington pits,) and the Seaton Delaval Coal Co. There were other concerns, such as Choppington Collieries Ltd., the East Holywell Coal Co., the Hepscott Coal Co., the Netherton Colliery, the Newbiggin Colliery Co., and Joseph Laycock & Co., owners of Seghill Colliery, while Burradon Colliery was owned by the Burradon & Coxlodge Coal Co. which also owned Hazlerigg and Killingworth 'Lizzie' pits.

The Blyth & Tyne was paralleled by the Cramlington and Backworth railways all the way from Seghill to Percy Main. At Holywell the B&T and Cramlington railways ran side by side giving the impression of a four-track railway.

The approach to Percy Main became a railway "spaghetti junction" as the B&T and three colliery lines all vied to reach their own staiths. Near West Chirton, with Flatworth Engine on the west side and Murton Row on the east side, the Backworth Railway passed over the Blyth & Tyne and Cramlington lines to join its branch from Algernon Pit and Blue Bell pits, before going to its own staiths at Whitehill Point. The Seaton Burn wagonway came in from the north west to pass over the Cramlington Railway and run along the west side the B&T. From here to Percy Main North the Seaton Burn, B&T and Backworth Railway all ran alongside each other before diverging to their own staiths, the B&T passing over the Seaton Burn at Percy Main North. Meanwhile, the Cramlington Railway, which had deviated to the west at Flatworth Engine, rejoined the B&T alongside Percy Main engine shed before continuing to its own staiths.

Coal from Backworth Collieries is recorded as first being loaded on to a ship from the company's own staith with due ceremony in 1818 which may well mark the start of the Backworth Railway, although it seems unlikely that there had not been wagonways from Alergnon(1784) and Maude (1814) pits before then. Either way, by 1838 the Backworth Railway had been extended north as far as West Cramlington, making it a total length of about seven miles. In addition, it was shared by the East Holywell Coal Co. which had its own branch to Earsdon from East Holywell and Fenwick pits as well its own staith at Hay Hole.

The Cramlington Railway was opened by the Cramlington Coal Co. in 1823 and also ran around seven miles from Ann Pit, East Cramlington, to its own staith at Hay Hole. It was extended north to Shankhouse Pit by 1847, from Ann Pit to the Newcastle & Berwick line at West Cramlington Junction by 1849, west from Seghill to Dudley Colliery in 1854, and north from Shankhouse to Hartford Pit by 1866. In 1898 the line from Ann Pit to West Cramlington was rerouted to connect with the Backworth Railway.

The seven-mile Seaton Burn Wagonway originated as the

On the Backworth Railway, NCB Austerity 0-6-0ST No.4(Robert Stephenson & Hawthorns 7166 of 1944) crosses the Howdon Road-Tyne Commission Quay road while easing a train of empties away from the staiths sidings at Whitehill Point in March 1967. The line on the right descends to the TIC Railway near TIC No. 9 signal box. *Roger Holmes/Photos from the Fifties*

One of many main line locomotives to work out their days on North East colliery lines. NCB No. 2 Area 0-6-0ST No. 22 of the Hartley Main system originated with the Barry Railway in South Wales. When the Barry Railway was absorbed by the Great Western it became GWR No. 729. No information is provided as to the location of this picture but close study of large scale Ordnance Survey maps suggests that No. 22 is approaching Seghill on BR metals with a train from Seaton Delaval, thus explaining why it is displaying BR class F unfitted freight headlamps - although the track hardly appears to be of passenger line standard. If Seghill, the lines joining from the left will be from East Cramlington, Seghill and Dudley collieries. *Neville Stead collection*

Brunton & Shields Railway opened in 1826 to connect Brunton Pit, via Burradon, with the Tyne at Hay Hole. It was connected to newly opened Seaton Burn Colliery in 1837 by the Seaton Burn Coal Co.

Having sold its own 1838 Seaton Delaval-Seghill line to the Blyth & Tyne in the 1850s, the Seaton Delaval Coal Co. again had its own three-mile line from 1859 which went from Seaton Delaval Colliery to its new Forster Pit(later renamed New Delaval Colliery) and brickworks at Newsham, and from 1872 it had a branch to New Hartley Colliery.

Surmounting Prospect Hill was as much a problem for the colliery lines as the Blyth & Tyne and with gradients as steep as 1 in 25 they too were forced to use rope-worked inclines powered by stationary engines until eventually they were rebuilt to ease the gradients. The use of inclines is still reflected in some place names, such as Middle Engine.

When Ashington collieries were being developed in the 1860s, the Blyth & Tyne was yet to reach that far north and so they were connected to the NER Newcastle-Berwick main line at Pegswood, and would not be connected to the B&T, via the Newbiggin branch at Ashington, until 1886. As new pits opened at Woodhorn, Linton, Ellington and Lynemouth between 1894 and 1934, the Ashington Railway progressively extended to almost 13 route miles. It was further extended in 1954 when a 1¼-mile branch was laid from Linton to Longhirst drift mine. At Ashington were workshops and the engine shed for a large fleet of locomotives. The line through Linton to Lynemouth was fully signalled with signal boxes at Ashington and along the way. It had to be - it also carried passenger trains for colliery workers and was used by the main line company's trains. The system was so busy and movements so complex that in the 1950s the NCB considered building a modern hump marshalling yard at Woodhorn in a bid to streamline operations. In 1956 a full circle was achieved when the Lynemouth-Woodhorn section was laid to provide a more direct route to Ashington and BR for traffic from Britain's biggest coal washery which had just been completed at Lynemouth. The new line was double track and colour-light signalled from a new NCB panel signal box at Lynemouth. When new, the layout at Lynemouth was more akin to one of BR's big new marshalling yards than colliery sidings.

The Bedlington Coal Co.'s railway dated from 1821. Lines ran from Barrington(near Choppington,) Bedlington, and West Sleekburn collieries to a staith on the Blyth. The Bedlington-Choppington section became part of the Blyth & Tyne's Morpeth branch in 1857.

A significant line was added in 1912 when the Hazlerigg

Ex-BR Class 14 Paxman 0-6-0 diesel hydraulic NCB No. 506(formerly BR No. D9504) passes closed Woodhorn Colliery as it heads a train for New Moor on Saturday 7th June 1986. *Neville Stead*

& Burradon Coal Co. laid the Burradon & Holywell Wagonway connecting the Seaton Burn Wagonway in the west with the Blyth & Tyne at Holywell Junction in the east. It gave the company direct locomotive-worked access to Northumberland Dock in place of the rope-worked Seaton Burn route which consequently fell out of use south of Hillhead Engine(Burradon) during the 1920s. The Burradon & Holywell would go on to become the last steam-worked colliery line in Northumberland

As the first half of the 20th century passed, agreements, mergers and general consolidations, in part influenced by war and economic depression, brought changes in ownership and rationalisation.

In 1929 the Cramlington and Seaton Delaval companies merged to form Hartley Main Collieries Ltd., one of Northumberland's largest and most acquisitive mining concerns. A programme of rationalisation and modernisation included a new mechanised loading facility at Howdon-on-Tyne built in partnership with the TIC and capable of loading two colliers simultaneously. Also in 1929 the Hazlerigg & Burradon Coal Co. took over Burradon Colliery from the Burradon & Coxlodge Coal Co. while in 1933 the East Holywell Coal Co.was absorbed by Backworth Collieries. Then in 1938, Hartley Main acquired the Seaton Burn Coal Co. and the Killingworth Railway By the time the coal industry was nationalized on 1st January 1947, the principal colliery systems which concern us here that were vested in the National Coal Board had been simplified into the Ashington Coal Co. railways, the Backworth Railway, and the Hartley Main Collieries railways, along with those of the Bedlington Coal Co., the Cowpen Coal Co., the Hazlerigg & Burradon Coal Co., the Netherton Coal Co., and Seghill Colliery.

At that time the Backworth system extended from Backworth 'C' Pit and Hotspur Brickworks, near Seghill (the old wagonway north of there to West Cramlington being long since abandoned,) through Backworth Colliery (Eccles, Maude and 'A' pits,) to a junction at Percy Main with the TIC line to the staiths at Whitehill Point, and to the Backworth Staiths at Northumberland Dock. It also comprised the branches from East Holywell Colliery('C' and Fenwick pits) and Church Pit which crossed the B&T on the level at Holywell, and also that from Algernon Colliery and Shiremoor which joined the main line at Murton Row. The workshops and engine shed were at Eccles Colliery.

At over 23 route miles the Hartley Collieries system was the most extensive with three groups of lines separate from each other. The former Cramlington Railway ran from Hartford Colliery(west of Newsham,) across the path of the old Plessey Wagonway, then past Shankhouse, Seghill, Holywell, Murton Row and Percy Main before dividing onto its own Howdon and Northumberland Dock staiths. Branches came into Shankhouse from Nelson Colliery, from Cramlington Ann Pit to a point between Shankhouse and Seghill, and to Seghill from Dudley Colliery where it also had an outlet onto the East Coast main line. The surviving former Seaton Burn and Killingworth lines extended from Burradon to West Moor Colliery and a connection with the East Coast main line at Killingworth, and over the ECML via Weetslade Colliery to Seaton Burn and Dinnington collieries. The former Seaton Delaval lines came from New Delaval Colliery and New Hartley collieries to Seaton Delaval where the central workshops and locomotive repair shop were located. The company's large motive power fleet included tender engines and ex-main line locomotives. Sections of the Seaton Burn and Killingworth lines were maintained at the time by the Hazlerigg & Burradon company. They were remote from the Blyth & Tyne but connected to it by the Burradon & Holywell line.

Passenger services

Besides the frequent electric services on the North Tyne Loop, the passenger service over former B&T metals at the end of the NER era consisted of trains between Manors North, Bedlington and Morpeth, between Monkseaton and Blyth(no Sunday service,) supplemented by more trains with a Sunday service between Newsham and Blyth making a total of 34 trains in and out of Blyth on weekdays(35 on Wednesdays and Saturdays,) and around 18 Bedlington-Ashington-Newbiggin trains each way on weekdays plus a reasonable Sunday service. There were also two non-stop trains each way between Newcastle Central and Blyth.

Service patterns were changed during the LNER era with the Manors-Morpeth service having ceased before the second world war, the 1939 timetable showing the Manors service running to/from Newbiggin and the Morpeth line being served by an infrequent Blyth-Morpeth 'Rail Motor' service. The term 'Rail Motor' could mean either a steam push-pull or a Sentinel steam railcar.

Early in the BR era, the non-electric service had been radically altered again with regular passenger services withdrawn from the Bedlington-Morpeth section from 3rd April 1950. The remaining services from June 1950 comprised eleven Manors to Newbiggin trains(the first train of the day being the 5.30am mails from Newcastle Central) and 10 Newbiggin to Manors plus extras on Saturdays while all five Sunday trains each way ran to/from Newcastle Central. There was one Monday-Saturday train from Blyth to Manors, at 11.56am. Trains on this route mostly ran non-stop between Manors and Backworth. Eight trains ran each way between Monkseaton and Blyth

Newsham was a key junction on the Blyth & Tyne, being where the original main line between Blyth station and Percy Main was joined by the extension from Bedlington and beyond, as well as branches from Isabella colliery and Blyth South Staiths. And with up to 30 departures every weekday in the 1950s, it was a fairly busy passenger interchange too. In 2016 it is no longer a junction other than where the singled line from Tyneside becomes double again but remains important as the run-round point for freight trains between North Blyth and the North via Morpeth. In this view, South Blyth's G5 0-4-4T No. 67323 prepares to propel its Newbiggin to Monkseaton push-pull service out of the station. The signals on the extreme left control the lines coming in from Blyth. *Neville Stead collection*

13

with two extra on Saturdays but there was no Sunday service. A further 12 Monday-Friday trains ran from Newsham to Blyth with seven from Blyth to Newsham plus extras on Wednesdays and Saturdays. They included three Blyth-Newbiggin trains each way which reversed at Newsham.

The summer 1955 working timetable reveals a further change in emphasis. The principal link with Newcastle was now via a change into the electric service at Monkseaton. The number of Monday-Friday trains via the Avenue Branch had increased to 14 each way, some running to/from Newbiggin as well as Blyth. The service varied considerably on Saturdays. The direct service to/from Manors had been drastically reduced with only two mid-week trains each way: the 5.30am mails from Newcastle Central - all stations from Benton including an unadvertised stop at Seghill - and the 5.20pm Manors-Newbiggin. In the opposite direction were the 7.37am Newbiggin-Manors and 6.35pm Newbiggin-Newcastle Central, presumably the return workings of the outward trains. On Saturdays, however, six trains ran in each direction including late evening departures from Manors. The Newsham-Blyth shuttle remained similar to 1950.

North Blyth was not, of course, served by passenger trains but it is worth mentioning that a chain ferry across the harbour, known as the 'High Ferry' provided a link with trains at Blyth.

All services on the Blyth & Tyne ran as class B ordinary passenger trains and, with the exception of the Manors and Newcastle trains, most were push-pull - 'Rail Motor'-operated. Services that were not were intended to convey parcels vans, horse boxes and carriage trucks, such trains between Blyth and Newbiggin being allowed seven minutes at Newsham for the engine to run round. The only Sunday train on the whole network now was the 11.59pm (Saturday) Blyth-Newbiggin plus empty stock workings from Newbiggin to Blyth at 12.27 and 12.45am.

The only timetabled class A express passenger train traversing the Blyth & Tyne was the summer Saturday Tynemouth-Glasgow which in 1955 ran from 16th July until 13th August. It was booked to call at Bedlington 11.52-54 to pick up only.

Steam was replaced by diesel multiple units on Blyth & Tyne services in 1958 but the emphasis on routes remained much the same with more trains than ever on the Monkseaton leg. The 1962 timetable shows 17 trains each way on Mondays to Fridays, mainly hourly and running alternately to/from Blyth and Newbiggin and departing Monkseaton at 33 minutes past the hour for much of the day. The service on the Manors leg, however, was no better than in 1955 while the 5.30am mails from Newcastle Central to Newbiggin and its 7.35am return remained loco-

Blyth & Tyne local services were once worked by Sentinel steam railcars as well as push-pull sets. Viewed from the Blyth platform at Newsham in the 1930s, LNER No. 2257 *Defiance* passes London Midland & Scottish Railway wagons in the sidings.
Neville Stead collection

During the 1950s and 60s the main route for passengers between Newbiggin, Blyth and Newcastle was via a change into the electric services at Monkseaton. G5 0-4-4T No. 67340 stands at Monkseaton in the 1950s with a push-pull set from Blyth. The engine has gained an extension to its side tanks but has lost a buffer along the way - which may be why it has hauled the train instead of propelling it.
Neville Stead collection

hauled. As in steam days, there were more trains along this route on Saturdays. An even more frequent service of Newsham-Blyth shuttles provided connections with Newbiggin trains, but the Blyth-Newbiggin service was by now reduced to one from Newbiggin and two from Blyth.

When DMUs took over, their limited space for carrying parcels required that a network of dedicated parcels trains be introduced to carry the traffic previously accommodated in vans attached to passenger trains. In 1960 parcels trains on the Blyth & Tyne consisted of the 9.40am and 3.18pm Newcastle Central-Monkseaton-Blyth-Newbiggin, and the 12.20pm(12.22 on Saturdays) and 6.18pm(6.5 on Saturdays) Newbiggin-Monkseaton.

The benefits of diesel operation could not save the Blyth & Tyne services and they were among early casualties of the Beeching era purges. The Monkseaton leg was withdrawn on 9th December 1963 and services between Manors, Newsham, Blyth and Newbiggin on 2nd November 1964, the last train being the 11.59pm Blyth-Newbiggin on Saturday 31st October. After withdrawal of regular services, the B&T continued to see occasional excursions and East Coast main line passenger trains diverted due to engineering work or blockages between Newcastle and Morpeth.

Further retrenchment came in June 1967 when the North Tyne Loop, including the former B&T section, was de-electrified and fully turned over to diesel operation. Things

looked even more bleak in 1973 when a report for the Tyne & Wear PTE suggested closing the line and turning it into a guided busway. In the event, common sense prevailed and since August 1980, it has formed a key part of the very busy and successful Newcastle Metro, again electrified, this time on 1500 volts dc overhead wires.

Not to be overlooked are the boat trains serving Tyne Commission Quay, which in summer included The Norseman from and to London King's Cross. They travelled to/from Newcastle Central via North Shields and the curve to Percy Main North where the engine had to run round its train before heading onto the T.I.C. Railway. The timetable for these was always complex with trains running at different times on different days of the week to fit in with the ferries. As a sample, on Friday August 12th 1955 the service would have consisted of empty stock workings from Heaton arriving at Tyne Commission Quay at 7.15, 7.35, 9.55 and 10.15am with corresponding departures of trains to Newcastle Central at 8.6 and 10.20am and to London King's Cross at 8.55 and 11am.

Arrivals were 2.3pm from Newcastle Central and 2.40pm from King's Cross, the empty stock being hauled off to Heaton at 3.4 and 3.50pm. A note in the Working Timetable stated that "empty trains from Tyne Commission Quay to Heaton carriage sidings may convey passengers to Walker Gate when required and will then be signalled class A"

At the beginning of 1969 through services between Tyne

A two-car Metro-Cammell DMU waits to leave Newbiggin-by-the-Sea with a Saturday service to Manors on 13th October 1962. The modern, cleaner and more efficient DMU's could not save the Blyth & Tyne passenger service and Newbiggin station was closed completely with effect from 2nd November 1964. *Chris Gammell/Photos from the Fifties*

Commission Quay and King's Cross ended, BR blaming a shortage of locomotives with the appropriate route availability that were capable of working modern air-braked coaches between the quay and Newcastle Central. A DMU connection was then run but that too was withdrawn on 2nd May 1970.

Whether a regular passenger service will return to the Blyth & Tyne in this new age of railways has been a long-running saga. Despite 20 years of repeated feasibility studies, the Ashington/Blyth-Newcastle passenger service has still not been reinstated. As recently as 2013 a £750,000 study was commissioned by Northumbria County Council. In March 2015, however, the reintroduction of services moved a step closer when news broke that the Department for Transport's tender document for re-letting of the Northern franchise set out an "expectation" that the new operator will support reinstatement of the Blyth & Tyne passenger service. Alongside this a pledge by Northumbria County Council to invest £350 million in capital projects included the B&T service. A target date of 2019 has been set with hourly Ashington-Newcastle trains, running half-hourly at peak times but leaving paths for existing and new freight traffic.

Freight

While general freight was carried to and from the various wayside stations and private sidings, coal was far and away the dominant traffic, though the considerable business in imported timber and pit props should not be overlooked. Coal was what the line was built for and remains dominant in 2016 - albeit in a very different context.

Much of this ceaseless coal traffic was internal to the B&T, being conveyed from the numerous pits within the area to staiths at Blyth and Percy Main, and in later years to the power station at Blyth Cambois. Practically every freight train on the system was arranged locally according to Mineral Leading practice involving close co-operation between the railway, collieries and ports and using dedicated resources such as engines, wagons and crews - a system used since the early 20th century.

So important was the B&T's coal traffic that in 1903 the NER, always innovative, introduced dedicated block trains composed of 25 40-ton bogie hopper wagons operating solely between Ashington and Blyth, a fore-runner of today's high capacity coal trains. After West Blyth staiths were completed in 1928, the annual tonnage being shipped through Blyth quickly rose to almost six million.

Subsequently coal was carried to the staiths in the ubiquitous standard 21-ton hopper wagons. By the early 1960s West Blyth staiths had been upgraded to take 24-ton wagons and were again upgraded for the air-braked 32-ton hoppers. By the 1980s these were becoming standard and widely used on the Merry-Go-Round system where trains could be loaded from giant bunkers at collieries and discharged automatically at power stations without even stopping.

As the local pits closed coal increasingly came to Blyth from sources outside the area, and from the 1980s in a procession of class 56-hauled MGR trains from such mines as Easington on the Durham coast and the opencast sites at Widdrington, Butterwell and Swalwell. It either went to the Cambois A and B power stations, opened in 1960 and 1966 respectively, or to the staiths for shipping to Thames power stations and export, mainly to Scandinavia. Coal also left the B&T by rail for destinations further afield, such as Wilton power station on Teesside.

Movements between North Blyth and the Morpeth direction had always involved a reversal at Bedlington's Furnace Way sidings - their name testimony to the erstwhile Bedlington Iron Company's works, though in more recent times they have usually reversed at Newsham. Trains also had to reverse at Morpeth until 1980 when BR laid the Morpeth North-Hepscott Curve which also saved a good deal of time for trains diverted from the ECML during engineering work or blockages between Morpeth and Newcastle. A proposed curve at Bedlington allowing trains to run direct between Morpeth and North Blyth has never come to pass.

The few booked freights featuring in the Working Timetable were all class H unfitted trains to and from Heaton yards or, after 1963, Tyne Yard.

In summer 1960 they were the 12.15am(not Mondays) Blyth-Heaton Up Yard, followed by the 12 noon North Blyth to Heaton Up Yard which returned untimed in the late afternoon from Heaton North Yard to Ashington Colliery; the 1.45pm from Heaton North Yard to Morpeth which was booked to stand or shunt at Newsham, Bedlington, Choppington, and at Hepscott when required; and the 7.45pm Lynemouth Colliery to Heaton Up Yard. Besides these, several trips a day between Percy Main and Heaton yards were listed in the Working Timetable.

So far as railways are concerned, Blyth is unusual in that it reached its peak in the 1960s. In 1961 just short of 6.9 million tons were shipped from Blyth, making it Europe's number one coal port. Soon after that, however, a gradual decline set in and Blyth would have to adapt to radically changing circumstances if it and its railway were to survive.

The decline was offset by the arrival of a major new industry - the Alcan aluminium smelter established in 1971, along with its own power station at Lynemouth and a berth at North Blyth for the unloading of ships bringing coke and the raw material, imported alumina. Besides a daily trainload to South Wales of outgoing aluminium ingots, were two return trips a day taking alumina from the import berth to the smelter. Alumina was also carried to Alcan's other plant at Fort William, and ingots from Fort William to

Standard everyday fayre on the Blyth & Tyne. Block coal trains formed of 21-ton hopper wagons and hauled by sturdy J27 0-6-0s. Nos. 65795(left) and 65834 pass at Freeman's Crossing on the Cambois branch. *Neville Stead collection*

17

Lynemouth. Coal required for the power station was fed directly by conveyor from Lynemouth Washery.

Another new freight run began in 1987 when three or four trains a week of containerised house coal began running from North Blyth Dock Sidings to Ellesmere Port with Ellington coal from Lynemouth for shipping to Northern Ireland. Apart from the pleasing sight for photographers of yellow Cawoods containers running behind a blue class 56, this traffic is memorable for being a break from the by then monotonous procession of MGR coal trains. British Coal retained two Barclay 0-6-0 diesels at Lynemouth for shunting the container wagons during loading. Following closure of Ellington mine in 1994, the traffic was switched to Gascoigne Wood in the Selby coalfield, and Barclay diesel No. 615 went with it to become the last standard gauge locomotive to work at a deep mine in the UK.

In March 2012 the aluminium smelter closed with the loss of over 500 jobs due to what Rio-Tinto Alcan described as "spiralling energy costs" - especially in the light of a new European directive on emissions. This resulted in the end of the North Blyth-Lynemouth alumina workings - the daily ingots train had ceased in 2009. The coal-fired power station remained in business under new ownership until December 2015 when it closed for conversion to biomass.

The closure of all the local pits from the 1970s to the 1990s, of Cambois power station in 2001 and the aluminum smelter, plus a shift to the new Tyne Coal Terminal established at Tyne Dock in 1985, have seen a steady reduction in traffic on B&T metals. It has survived, but nowadays it is imported coal coming in through Blyth instead of exports that is being carried. The number of trains, however, bears no resemblance to the constant coal movements of the past though another reason for fewer trains is that today's loaded coal trains weigh 2,200 tonnes apiece, the equivalent of two MGR trains.

Even so, in June 2015 there were less than ten trains per 24 hours, these days booked in the Working Timetable as they travel well beyond B&T limits and have to be pathed over busy passenger lines. As well as the North Blyth-Fort William alumina train reversing at Newsham and running via Morpeth, these consisted of loaded coal trains from North Blyth to the Yorkshire and Trent Valley power stations with corresponding empties, some coming from the Tyne Coal Terminal or Doncaster. The Working Timetable also had paths for two daily Tyne Coal Terminal-Lynemouth power station loaded coal trains with returning empties which were cancelled at the time.

Even this modern scene is now just a memory. The chimneys of Lynemouth aluminium works and power station dominate the skyline as English Welsh & Scottish Railway Type 5 No. 66217 passes Hirst Lane and approaches Ashington with empty alumina tanks for North Blyth at 16.03 on Tuesday 6th September 2005. No trace remains of the NCB line that continued to the left. *Stephen Chapman*

All change

The Beeching era brought an immediate change to both BR and NCB lines at both ends of the system. The northern extremity was lost upon withdrawal by BR of public passenger and freight services from the Woodhorn-Newbiggin section in November 1964. This necessitated the NCB having to lay a new 1 1/4-mile line from Lynemouth to serve Newbiggin Colliery, although the BR line continued to serve the colliery, worked under "One Engine in Steam" arrangements, until being finally abandoned in 1965. The new line lasted little over two years as Newbiggin Colliery itself closed in 1967.

But the Newbiggin branch was a minor loss compared to what happened further south between 1964 and the early 1970s. Between those years, all railway on the south bank of the River Blyth - a complex network of three lines through the town serving Isabella, Cowpen, Crofton Mill and Bates collieries, a passenger station, coal staiths, docks, warehouses. dry docks, fish quay and South Blyth engine shed, was wiped out except for the BR and NCB lines necessary to serve the remaining pit and coal wharf at Bates.

Rationalisation also took place at North Blyth with the closure of Cambois Colliery, its staiths and BR's North Blyth staiths in 1968. With the end of BR steam working in September 1967 the twin engine sheds at North and South Blyth were replaced by a new diesel depot at Cambois which became the main operating centre for the Blyth & Tyne.

At the Tyne end of the system, the railway retrenchment from Percy Main began back in 1960 when the Hartley Main line closed, followed in 1969 by the Backworth Railway, leaving only the BR line. In 1970 the passenger trains to Tyne Commission Quay ended and by that same year the coal staiths were all out of use or dismantled, leaving just sidings and lines to Albert Edward Dock, ultimately served by just a single line from Percy Main North. A new rail-connected Esso oil terminal was established at Percy Main but the spur into Albert Edward Dock was by then the only other remaining railway. In 1975 it was reported that rail traffic at the dock had all but ended, and the early 1980s saw the removal of all remaining track south of Earsdon Junction. The whole dock area has since been replaced by the marinas, houses and shops that make up the Royal Quays development. Ferries still sail to Scandinavia and Northern Europe from the International Ferry Terminal on the riverside at Whitehill Point.

Throughout the 1970s, the northern end of the B&T continued to function almost in a world of its own, virtually detached from the many changes underway on the rest of BR. Its trains, like blood pumped through veins from its beating heart at Cambois, retraced their steps daily back and forth between the various pits, the staiths, the power station and the Alcan smelter at Lynemouth.

In the early 1980s BR spent £750,000 on modernising West Blyth staiths, including the installation of modern

An expanse of railway at Blyth, all gone by the 1970s. The view is towards Newsham on Saturday 17th May 1958 with South Blyth engine shed on the right and Blyth Crossing signal box in the centre. The cattle dock is on the left while J27 No. 65800 is standing on the line that went to Isabella via Cowpen "A' Pit. *Neville Stead collection*

conveyors which could deliver and trim the coal to the exact required position in the ship's hold. But it was in vain - the wheel had come full circle because again the staiths could not deal with larger vessels by then in use. The Opencast Executive of British Coal(to which the NCB was renamed in 1988) withdrew the support which it had granted towards the staiths' upkeep. West Blyth staiths were closed, the last shipment taking place on 31st December 1989 from what were the last timber staiths in use by BR.

This was not the end of rail-fed coal shipments - far from it. The Opencast Executive bought the disused Newsham North Junction-Isabella branch from BR, had the whole route to the site of closed Bates Colliery rebuilt, and installed a new MGR-discharge and deep water shiploading facility capable of accommodating vessels of up to 25,000 tonnes. It also had a large stockpile area which was a great benefit to the railway as trains could discharge without having to wait for ships to be ready. Trains began carrying coal from various opencast sites to Bates in spring 1991 after several months of deliveries by road. Unfortunately the Bates operation was relatively short-lived as railborne coal shipments from all the North East were eventually concentrated on the new terminal at Tyne Dock which had opened in 1985. The last train ran to Bates in 2000, the rail connection being finally removed in 2008.

As with the main line railways, the coal industry would undergo great change following nationalisation in 1947 and already many of the pits in the area were seen as having a limited life, while investment would be concentrated mainly on the most modern and productive ones, most notably Lynemouth and Ellington. But unlike BR, change would ultimately end with extinction of both the collieries and their railways.

Apart from unexpected occurances which can bring about the sudden death or reduction of a viable mine - insurmountable geological difficulties, roof falls, flood, fire or just plain worked out - demand for coal was starting to fall in the 1950s, not least as BR turned from steam to diesel traction and industry to electricity, the effects of clean air legislation, and the discovery of North Sea gas in the 1960s which eliminated the use of coal for making gas. Balanced against this were big new power stations being built to meet the evermore voracious demand for electricity and big efficiency improvements from BR and the coal industry alike were required in order to meet their needs. The change to Merry-Go-Round operation by BR brought a huge improvement in efficiency, the train effectively acting as a conveyer belt between pit and power station. But as collieries converted to this system their own internal railways and locomotives were no longer needed.

One by one the pits had been closing since the 1950s and, inevitably, their railways were abandoned. In 1960,

As one door closed another opened. Railborne coal began running to the new automatic discharge and ship loading terminal on the site of Bates Colliery in 1991. On the first day of rail operation, Monday 8th April, Type 5 No. 56127, nicely scrubbed up in British Rail Trainload Coal sub-sector livery, eases a fully loaded MGR working from Butterwell through the discharge point. *Stephen Chapman*

Seaton Delaval Colliery, which at its peak employed over 3000 men, closed and the former Hartley Collieries main line to Percy Main with it. Seaton Delaval workshops also closed, their work and staff transferred to new Central Workshops at Ashington which had opened in 1959, replacing older shops at Ashington, Linton and Cowpen collieries. The new shops were the biggest on the NCB with a million square feet of covered floor space and at their height employed over 1000 workers repairing and manufacturing all kinds of colliery equipment, including surface and underground locomotives and wagons.

The regular use of steam traction would not be eliminated from the NCB's Northumberland Area until the end of 1975 but the process of modernisation had been gathering pace since the 1950s, first with the replacement of venerable steam locomotives - the Hartley Main tender engines being among them - by more modern powerful 0-6-0 saddle tanks, the ubiquitous Austerities in particular. In January 1969 the end of steam was foretold when D9511, the first of the Paxman Class 14 diesels to be bought from BR, arrived at Ashington loco shed with which they would become synonymous. Over the ensuing years more arrived to replace steam on NCB lines throughout the area, such as at Burradon, and at Backworth where they enabled withdrawal of the area's last working steam locomotives.

The Backworth Railway was severely truncated in 1969 with closure of the whole line to Northumberland Dock from just south of Eccles Colliery, where a short section across the B1322 road remained as a headshunt for the exchange sidings with BR and the Fenwick Colliery branch. BR's B&T line was now the only railway going to Percy Main where there were once four.

By this time, most of the Ashington Railway loop to Ellington via Linton was disused, the passenger service having ceased in May 1966. The Ellington-Lynemouth section became redundant when Ellington pit and Bewick Drift mine began sending their output to Lynemouth Washery by conveyor.

The Bedlington system had gone by 1971 when Bedlington Colliery itself closed, West Sleekburn pit having closed in 1962. The former Cowpen Coal Company's railways were much reduced during the 1960s upon closure of North Seaton Colliery in 1961 and Cambois in 1968. Although Isabella pit closed in 1966 the railway still served Bates.

The 1970s gave us the impression that the coal industry now had a strong future although its railways would continue to contract due in no small measure to the expansion of MGR working. By 1973 there were just eight rail-served collieries in the area referred to by this book. After the 1974 miners' strike, the new Labour government set about modernising the more viable pits. In 1975 the NCB wharf at Bates was shipping around 7000 tons a day. Besides the colliery's own production, coal was brought from local pits by BR to Isabella Sidings from where it was taken over the NCB line to Bates, the NCB still needing up to three of its own locomotives working per shift to deal with the traffic. Even so, pits continued to close. Netherton

The Hartley Main was one of those notable North East colliery systems which used tender engines, some ex-main line and some built purely for industrial service, like No. 6(built by Robert Stephenson & Co. in 1899, works No. 2917) seen at Seaton Delaval Colliery on Wednesday 12th June 1957. *Neville Stead collection*

Colliery and its mile-long branch from Choppington, the last vestige of the Netherton Coal Company's system, closed in 1975, Dudley Colliery - the last Hartley Main remnant for many years connected only to the East Coast main line - closed in 1977, as did the former Burradon & Holywell line. Fenwick Colliery closed in 1973 and what then remained of the Backworth Railway in July1980 upon closure of Eccles Colliery.

Opencast - or surface mining - had been developing further north, at Widdrington and then the big new site at Butterwell for which new railways were built. The Ashington-Linton portion of the closed NCB Ashington-Lynemouth loop was reopened in 1978 as part of a direct line from Butterwell to the B&T at Ashington for use by BR trains. The lines from Lynemouth to Ashington and Ashington to Butterwell were now just about all that remained of this once extensive system.

The 1980s will go down in history as a catastrophic decade for the coal industry with the national strike of 1984/85 aimed at fighting the government's Draconian pit closure programme. Immediately the strike was over the closure of Bates Colliery was announced and the last rail traffic ran on 23rd April 1986 when BR removed remaining wagons from Isabella Sidings. Ashington Washery closed in December, leaving the Ashington loco fleet with little more to do than shift coal from Lynemouth to the New Moor stockpile next to the Butterwell line. This ended in March 1987 when the Ashington system ceased internal operations and Ashington engine shed closed. Reports started to filter through of the astonishing sight of a thousand NCB wagons stored in row upon row at New Moor. But the only coal trains on the NCB's lines now were run by BR, from Lynemouth and Butterwell. Ashington Colliery itself closed in March 1988. Ashington workshops continued in business for a few more years, having been redesignated "Area National Workshop" in 1985 but no longer rail-connected; standard gauge locomotives had been repaired at Lambton Engine Works, County Durham, since 1975 anyway.

In 1993 the newly-privatised power generators awarded their contracts for coal supply and most of it would now be imported from overseas, spelling the end for many of the mines which had survived the 1980s. In early 1994 it looked to be all over for Northumberland deep mining when British Coal closed the Ellington Combined Mine - into which Ellington, the Bewick Drift and Lynemouth had been merged in 1983. Upon privatisation of the industry Ellington was taken over by R. J. B. Mining and reopened in 1995, gaining another 10 years' life.

For the railway, the Ellington closure had been a veiled blessing because all Lynemouth power station's coal now had to be brought from a variety of other sources including Redcar, Hunterston and Tyne Dock import terminals, and

Rows and rows of NCB wagons await their fate at New Moor in 1986 upon impending closure of the Ashington system. *Adrian Booth*

Butterwell, Widdrington and Killoch(Ayrshire) opencasts. For this a rail unloading facility was installed in 1996.

Even so, local traffic had declined massively, leading to the closure of Cambois depot in 1996. Cambois power stations closed in 2001 and then, early in 2005 national news headlines reported serious underground flooding at Ellington. This time the pit closed for good - the last deep coal mine in the North East, bringing to an end the industry which had defined the whole region.

If the port of Blyth and the railway serving it were to survive they had to adapt to the new age of imported coal, and in 2006 an import terminal was opened at Battleship Wharf, North Blyth. Since then, coal has come in through Blyth instead of going out.

In February 2010, the Ashington-Butterwell light railway, then owned by UK Coal, was abandoned, trains removing coal from a new opencast site at Potland using the East Coast main line outlet from Butterwell.

The Woodhorn-Lynemouth section of the Ashington Railway, transferred to Alcan ownership in 1994, survived for use by main line trains taking coal to the power station. However, at the time of writing in early 2016, the power station, now owned by Lynemouth Power, was closed for conversion to burning biomass and all coal trains to Lynemouth were cancelled, leaving the line from West Sleekburn Junction to Ashington and Lynemouth with no booked traffic. Whether the biomass will be delivered by rail or road remains to be seen.

All that remains now of Northumberland's intense deep mining industry is a museum at the former Woodhorn Colliery. One other section of the once dense network of mineral railways survives, however, and now we can ride on it. That is two miles of single track from Middle Engine to Percy Main. Part was resurrected in 1975 as a test track for new Metro cars until 1981when it had fulfiled its purpose and was then preserved as the Stephenson Railway Museum, now the North Tyneside Steam Railway.

B&T supporters can at least feel reassured by one dramatic change - the re-electrification and conversion in the late 1970s of the Newcastle-Monkseaton section to the the busy and successful Metro.

Apart from being whittled away at the extremities - Percy Main, Newbiggin and Blyth - the Blyth & Tyne remains just about intact in 2016 and continues to be available as a diversionary route for the East Coast main line. But it is now only a single line all the way from Newsham to Benton East where it is no longer connected to the Newcastle-Monkseaton line since its conversion to Metro. Nowadays it passes, double track, underneath it to join the East Coast main line at Benton Quarry Junction.

The B&T has survived many challenges but in 2015 a new threat arose. That was the doubling of the UK carbon tax - known technically as the Carbon Floor Price - in order to speed up the reduction of CO_2 emissions. This especially increases the cost of burning coal and, along with other factors, has already caused Ferrybridge coal-fired power station in Yorkshire to close. Others are sure to follow. The writing is on the wall for coal-fired power stations anyway and, consequently, the trains that deliver the coal from places like Blyth. It is very likely that the B&T's long-term future may be entirely dependent on a resumption of passenger services.

Preserved Sulzer Type 2 No. 24061 *Experiment* **passes West Chirton in 1993 while heading north on the North Tyne Steam Railway, a lasting reminder of the once bustling railway on the approach to Percy Main.** *Neville Stead*

MANORS NORTH-MONKSEATON

ABOVE: The east end bay platforms at Newcastle Central, since 1909 the starting point for a journey over erstwhile Blyth & Tyne metals to Monkseaton. In early BR days, one of the electric units introduced by the LNER in 1937 awaits its next departure. *Tom Greaves*

BELOW: In 1909 when the NER completed its new electrified route to Newcastle Central, it included a new through station at Manors North, replacing the original Blyth & Tyne terminus at New Bridge Street which became a goods station. The new station included three north-facing bay platforms for Blyth and Newbiggin services, most of which still started there right until withdrawal in the 1960s. South Blyth G5 0-4-4T No. 67246 awaits departure from one of the bays with a Newbiggin train on 8th May 1954. *Neville Stead*

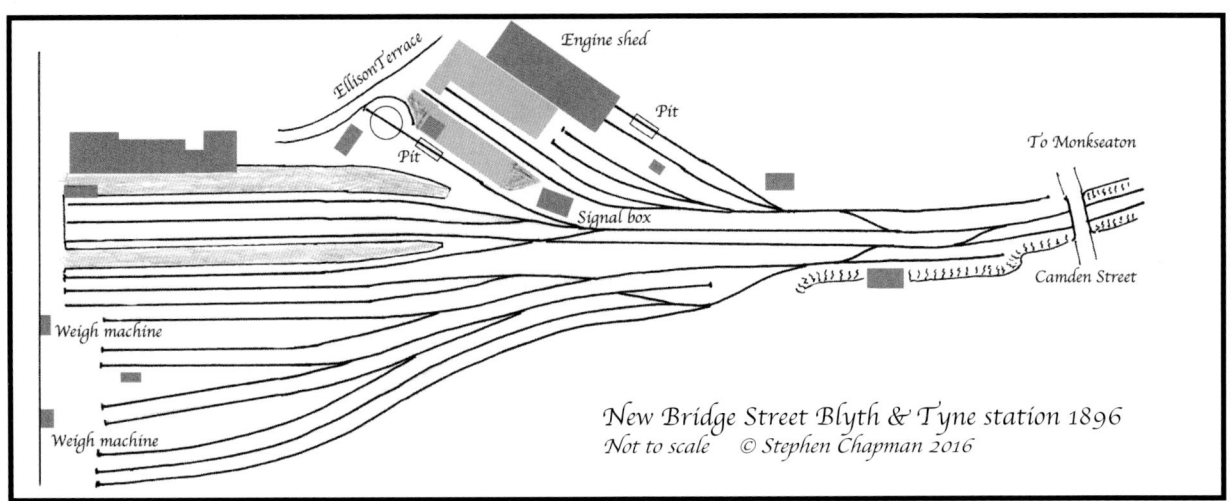

New Bridge Street Blyth & Tyne station 1896
Not to scale © Stephen Chapman 2016

MANORS JUNCTION TO MONKSEATON *British Railways N. E. Region Sectional Appendix 1960*

Signalling: Absolute Block. **Maximum speed on main lines:** 60mph
Additional running lines: Up refuge siding entered by facing points accommodating 34 wagons, engine and brake van at South Gosforth station; Up Goods loop at Killingworth accommodating 25 wagons, engine and brake;
Signal Boxes: Manors North(539yds from Manors Jn.,) Jesmond station(509yds.,) West Jesmond station (1718yds.,) South Gosforth station(1525yds.,) South Gosforth East(712yds.,) Benton station(1 mile 1051yds.,) Benton East(1005yds.,) Killingworth(559yds.,) Backworth(1 mile 853yds.,) Earsdon Grange(1 mile 415yds.,) Monkseaton West(1 mile 244yds.,) Monkseaton East(478yds.)
Gradients: 1in 254 falling from Manors Jn. to Manors North. 1 in 75 rising from Jesmond to South Gosforth.

The 1969 Sectional Appendix showed the signalling as Track Circuit Block and the only remaining signal boxes on this section were at South Gosforth and Monkseaton. The goods loop at Killingworth had been removed.

A Newcastle-bound stopping service with car E29127E leading pulls into South Gosforth station on Sunday 12th February 1967. The branch to Ponteland diverges left just through the bridge. The classic NER footbridge was still there in 2016, having survived conversion to the Metro and overhead electrification. *R. Patterson/Colour-Rail*

ABOVE: Freight on the Newcastle Metro. With South Gosforth car sheds, by this time the Metro depot, in the background, Brush Type 2 No. 31306 passes South Gosforth East Junction with a trip working from Rowntree's confectionery factory at Fawdon, on the Ponteland branch. The train will access the East Coast main line via the curve from Benton station to Benton Quarry Junction and continue through Newcastle Central to Tyne Yard. The date is Thursday 24th May 1984. *Neville Stead*

BELOW: The same working on Tuesday 8th October 1985 passing Benton station with Sulzer Type 2 No 25213 in charge. *Neville Stead*

ABOVE: Benton station in the 1960s with an EMU leaving for Newcastle. Benton had a small goods yard comprising two sidings which was situated on the left beyond the station. It was listed in 1956 as handling general goods and equipped with a 3-ton permanent crane.

BELOW: The intersection bridge east of Benton station where the Blyth & Tyne portion of the North Tyne Loop crosses over the Newcastle & Berwick portion of the East Coast main line. The EMU shows clearly the articulated bogie of the electric stock used on the North Tyne services. *Both Neville Stead collection*

ABOVE: In the late 1970s, the Inverness-York Motorail, diverted via the Blyth & Tyne, is about to regain the East Coast main line at Benton Quarry Junction whilst negotiating the curve from Benton East Junction. The engine is English Electric Type 4 No. 40086. At one time, between Benton East Junction and Backworth came the intersection and exchange sidings with the Killingworth Wagonway, followed by Benton Square passenger station which closed in 1915, and then the intersections with the Seaton Burn Wagonway and the Backworth Railway.

BELOW: A DMU from the coast pulls into Backworth station during the 1970s. The original Blyth & Tyne station buildings are on the right. The booking office on the overbridge is a later addition in a style which featured at a number of stations throughout the North East, including Seaton Delaval. There were no goods facilities at this station, these being at Holywell. Backworth station was closed and demolished upon conversion of the line to Metro, its B&T buildings being lost in the process. It was replaced by a new transport interchange further east called Shiremoor. The bridge carrying the Backworth Railway is behind the photographer. *Both Neville Stead*

ABOVE: Between 1860 and 1915 a series of changes in layout took place at Monkseaton. The first station, called Whitley, was well to the south on the original 1860 Blyth & Tyne route to Tynemouth. In 1864 when the line from Newcastle was opened, it was replaced by a new Whitley station immediately south of the level crossing with the Monkseaton-Whitley Park road(Marine Avenue.) The Newcastle line joined the original route at Whitley Junction, immediately north of the crossing. In 1882 when the NER completed the coastal line via Whitley Bay and Cullercoats, Whitley station was renamed Monkseaton and the original B&T route to Tynemouth closed. The present station seen here, situated immediately south west of the 1864 one, was completed in 1915 to deal with increased traffic resulting from electrification, and is situated on a new alignment laid to connect the Newcastle line with the 1882 coastal line; a spur was also laid from the Hartley branch to the new station. Until 1964, Monkseaton formed the interchange between the electric services and those from Blyth and Newbiggin. Articulated Sentinel steam railcar No. 2291 *Phenomena* waits the road with a late 1930s service to Blyth.

BELOW: V1 2-6-2T No. 67673 pulls out of Monkseaton with a parcels train to Newcastle via the coast on Thursday 30th August 1956. Being steam, it may well have originated at Blyth, having been shunted into the bay so that electric services could pass during loading/unloading. The rule was that vehicles without lamp brackets should not be marshalled at the end of a train but who cares when the tail lamp can be hung from the draw hook! *Both Neville Stead collection*

ABOVE: The carriage sidings in this 1938 view from the footbridge in the previous picture stand on what remained at Monkseaton of the original B&T route to Tynemouth. When the 1882 coastal line on the left was opened, the original line was abandoned beyond Whitleyhill Heads, marked by the line of houses crossing from left to right in the far distance. *Neville Stead collection*

BELOW: The same view in the late 1970s when the Monkseaton-Newcastle section was closed for conversion to the Metro. On this occasion, the date of which has gone unrecorded, English Electric Type 4 No. 40004 has brought the Gateshead breakdown crane via Wallsend and Tynemouth to retrieve a small dumper truck which late night revellers had pushed onto the line at Monkseaton station. *Neville Stead*

ABOVE: On Thursday 30th August 1956, G5 0-4-4T No. 67340 takes water in the sidings at Monkseaton between turns on Blyth services. As can be seen from the loading gauge and the mineral wagons in the distance, the truncated Blyth & Tyne route to Tynemouth was also used as a goods and coal yard. *This and picture below: Neville Stead collection*

BELOW: The Royal Train with H.M. The Queen on board brings out the crowds at the south end of Monkseaton station on the morning of 30th October 1954. V3 2-6-2Ts Nos. 67689 and 67653 are taking her to Newcastle via Whitley Bay after she spent the night on the Avenue(Hartley) branch. B1 4-6-0 No. 61019 *Nilghai* **and 67689 had taken the Royal Train there the previous evening, Monkseaton-Blyth services being diverted via Backworth for the duration of Her Majesty's overnight stay. The Avenue Branch was a regular Royal Train night halt. A point of interest is the detailed variation between the two locomotives, 67689 having straight steam pipes.**

ABOVE: Leaving Monkseaton, G5 0-4-4T No. 67340 heads a service to Blyth or Newbiggin along the single track Avenue Branch on Thursday 30th August 1956. *Neville Stead collection*

The 3 mile 1305-yard Avenue Branch from Monkseaton to Hartley was listed in the 1960 BR North Eastern Region Sectional Appendix as being single track signalled by electric token. There were no crossing loops or intermediate signal boxes between Monkseaton West and Hartley. The maximum line speed was 45mph. There was an intermediate siding just south of Hartley, called Avenue Siding to which the propelling of 10 freight wagons with or without a brake van was permitted from Hartley in daylight and clear weather. The siding was abandoned in the 1950s and this note was deleted from the Sectional Appendix per a supplement issued in March 1958. From Hartley to Dairy House the Avenue branch took the course of an earlier wagonway, the surviving portion of which to Seaton Sluice remained connected to the branch at least until the 1870s.

BELOW: The station that never was. Collywell Bay was to be the terminus of an electrified line off the Avenue branch at what would have been Brierdene Junction but construction was halted by the 1914-18 war and never resumed. This photograph dated 21st August 1964 shows how Collywell Bay station ended up, with pigeon lofts occupying the space between the platforms. *Neville Stead collection*

BACKWORTH-MORPETH

Originally, the core route of the Blyth & Tyne was between Percy Main and Blyth, but in more recent times the Sectional Appendix listed it as from Backworth Junction to Morpeth. This was the starting point at Backworth Junction with the 1864 Newcastle-Monkseaton line going to the right and the curve connecting it to the original Percy Main-Blyth route at Earsdon Junction going to the left. The overbridge carries the former Cramlington Railway as well as the Blyth & Tyne line to Percy Main.

The junction was abolished when the Newcastle-Monkseaton line was converted to Metro and nowadays a single line which has run alongside the Metro since Benton East diverges to the left. In 2005 Northumberland Park Metro station was opened on the site of Backworth station (behind the photographer) and should a Blyth passenger service be reinstated it will become an interchange between the two. *Neville Stead collection*

BACKWORTH TO MORPETH VIA SEGHILL
British Railways North Eastern Region Sectional Appendix October 1960

Signalling: Absolute Block Backworth-Choppington. Electric Token Choppington-Hepscott. No token Hepscott-Morpeth.

Maximum speed on main and single lines: 45mph

Additional running lines: Up and Down Goods Lines Newsham South - North

Signal Boxes: Backworth; Earsdon(617yds from Backworth;) Holywell(722yds;) Seghill South(1 mile 546yds;) Seghill North(396yds;) Seaton Delaval Station(1645yds;) Hartley Station(1 mile 410yds; Newsham South(1 mile 520yds;) Newsham North(683yds;) Bebside(1 mile 1516yds;) Bedlington South(1657yds;) Bedlington North(247yds;) Choppington Station(1 mile 636yds;) Hepscott Station(1 mile 694yds;) Morpeth Station(1 mile 427yds.)

Gradients: 1 in 103 rising to Holywell; 1 in 249 falling at Seghill;1 in 496 falling at Newsham.

The 1969 Sectional Appendix showed Backworth Signal Box abolished and the line to Earsdon as Track Circuit Block worked by Benton signal box. Seghill South, Seaton Delaval and Hartley boxes had also been abolished.

ABOVE: Earsdon Junction and Earsdon signal box looking north. Besides the junction between the Backworth(left) and Percy Main (foreground) lines the signalman had to deal with NCB trains on the East Holywell colliery branch from Backworth to Fenwick Pit which crossed the BR line(and the NCB's Hartley Main line - the former Cramlington Railway - out of sight on the left) on the level. This view shows an NCB Austerity 0-6-0ST heading over the flat crossing with internal wagons to Fenwick Colliery. *Neville Stead collection*

BELOW: English Electric Deltic Type 5 No. 55014 *The Duke of Wellington's Regiment* heads diverted King's Cross-Edinburgh sleeper 1S70 past Holywell signal box in the early morning sunshine on Sunday 22nd June 1980. *Neville Stead*

ABOVE: With the Burradon & Holywell line going left across the double track and fully signalled NCB Hartley Main line, Q6 0-8-0 No. 63359 rolls an Up class H coal train past Holywell Junction. Amidst all this coal, there was still room for general goods and on the right is Holywell's small goods yard which was equipped to handle general goods and livestock. The jib of its 1-ton crane is just visible. The original Backworth station was sited here. It closed in 1864 when the Manors-Monkseaton line opened, the goods yard being renamed Holywell. *Neville Stead collection*

RIGHT: The first passenger station 2 miles 500 yards north of Backworth Junction was Seghill which had only one platform, on the Up side, Down trains thus having to cross over to call there. This undated view looking north shows the platform, station building, Seghill North signal box and signals controlling the junction with the lines to Seghill Colliery and the Hartley Main system.
The late Rev. John Parker/ Photos from the Fifties

ABOVE: Viewed from Seghill station platform in 1967, Ivatt Class 4 2-6-0 No. 43123 heads a Down train of empty hoppers. The old NCB Hartley Main railway is still *in situ* on the right. *Roger Holmes/Photos from the Fifties*

BELOW: Just under a mile beyond Seghill was Seaton Delaval station seen here looking north in the late 1950s. The picture shows reconstruction of the overbridge, which previously carried a ticket office similar to that at Backworth on page 28. The bridge sustained damage from a defence installation during the second world war and needed extra supports on the Up line which had to be taken out of use as a result, all trains thus having to be routed over the Down line. The Up line was reinstated once the bridge reconstruction seen here was completed. The signal arm on the left controls access to Seaton Delaval Colliery.
The late Rev. John Parker/Photos from the Fifties

ABOVE: Seaton Delaval station looking south in the 1950s with a Manors-Newbiggin service approaching behind a V1 or V3 2-6-2T. The disused Up line, platform and severed crossover are on the left. *The late Rev. John Parker/Photos from the Fifties*

BELOW: By the start of the 1960s the Up line had been reinstated but the station was closed to passengers with effect from 2nd November 1964. Here, Jubilee 4-6-0 No. 45562 *Alberta*, all the way from Leeds Holbeck shed, heads through closed Seaton Delaval station with the northbound Ashington Railtour on Saturday 10th June 1967. The Blyth & Tyne has long been - and still is - a railtour favourite. *Neville Stead collection*

ABOVE: On Sunday 3rd July 1983, Brush Type 4 No. 47521 heads diverted sleeper service 1S77 past the site of Seaton Delaval goods siding, just north of the station with the site of the colliery on the right. In 1956 Seaton Delaval was listed as equipped to handle general goods, livestock and horse boxes and prize cattle vans. Goods facilities were withdrawn on 9th December 1963 but the skeleton of the one-ton permanent crane survives 20 years later. Within less than three years, the line had been singled and the old crane had gone.

BELOW: A sea of caravans occupies the site of Seaton Delaval Colliery, as Ruston-engined Type 3 No. 37906 passes by with the Lynemouth Alcan to Tees aluminium ingots train in 1986. Overlooking the caravans are the old Hartley Main workshops, the taller building being occupied by Dallas Carpets. The bare site of the goods yard is in the foreground. *Both Neville Stead*

ABOVE: J27 0-6-0 No. 65789 hauls an Up loaded train through Hartley station. Judging by the fact that the station nameboard on the extreme left has been removed, this undated scene may well be after closure. The recently rebuilt signal box is just visible through the trees, left of the station buildings beyond which was the Avenue Branch from Monkseaton. *Neville Stead collection*

BELOW: Another of the railtours attracted to the Blyth & Tyne was an RCTS special hauled from Leeds on Sunday 19th September 1965 by A4 Pacific No. 60004 *William Whitelaw*. This picture shows the Newcastle-Morpeth-Newcastle leg approaching Newsham South signal box with the Up and Down goods loops on each side at 15.51 hours behind Ivatt Class 4 2-6-0 No. 43057. Beyond the bushes on the left, Hannah Siding went off the Up loop to the site of Newsham Colliery which had closed as long ago as 1926. In 1956 the siding was listed as serving Messrs. R. Fraser & Son, R.R. Nixon, and Mrs. Hall. *Robert Anderson*

ABOVE: Being a useful diversionary route for the East Coast main line, the Blyth & Tyne can see express passenger trains of the highest order. In this view on Saturday 14th November 1992, during a serious blockage between Morpeth and Newcastle, Brush Type 4 No. 47567 drags the Up Flying Scotsman, the 08.30 Glasgow-King's Cross InterCity 225, past Newsham South signal box and on to the single line. Electric loco No. 91023 is on the rear. The previous picture was taken from this signal box. *Neville Stead*

BELOW: Brush Type 5 No. 60071 approaches Newsham South with the Lynemouth-Tees freight conveying aluminium ingots for South Wales at 16.05 on Monday 9th October 2006. *Stephen Chapman*

ABOVE: Newsham Change for Blyth proclaims the station nameboard as G5 0-4-4T No. 67261 propels a 3-coach push-pull service for Monkseaton out of the station and past Newsham North signal box on Friday 20th September 1957. Three was the maximum permitted number of vehicles which could be propelled on Blyth & Tyne push-pull services. *This and picture below: Neville Stead collection*

BELOW: Change for Blyth no more. Passenger services were axed on 2nd November 1964 and Newsham station now presents a grim scene. J27 0-6-0 No. 65811 threads an Up coal train comprising a mixed bag of wagons through the forlorn platforms on a dull Monday 1st August 1966. At least the station clock survives. Newsham's one long siding for local goods was on the left beyond the hut at the platform end. It was listed in 1956 as equipped to handle general goods and livestock with a 11/2-ton crane. It closed on 7th June 1965.

41

ABOVE: Bebside level crossing, signal box and station house with a Class 37 powering northbound on 31st July 1972. *Peter Rose*
Known as Cowpen Lane until 1860, Bebside Station closed to passengers when services were withdrawn on 2nd November 1964 and to goods on 9th December 1963. Its one goods siding was equipped to handle general traffic only and had no permanent crane. Bebside signal box ceased to be a block post per a supplement issued on 6th March 1976. Just right of here was Horton Grange Colliery which closed in 1962.

BELOW: Between Bebside and Bedlington the Blyth & Tyne crosses the River Blyth by means of Kittybrewster Viaduct, one of two impressive bridges which are the biggest structures on the route. This timeless scene shows preserved A4 Pacific No. 60009 *Union of South Africa* heading a Cleethorpes-Morpeth special on Saturday 19th May 2007. *Neville Stead*
It was from the shores visible in this picture that coal was shipped from the earliest wagonways and the remains of jetties are visible through the second span from left of the road bridge. Just showing above the third road bridge pier are the alumina silos of the North Blyth import facility.

RIGHT: The approach to Bedlington from the south is marked by Furnace Way Sidings, used mainly by trains reversing while running between Morpeth and North Blyth or Lynemouth. In this view General Motors Type 5 No. 66129 passes the sidings while en-route light engine from Tyne Yard to Lynemouth at 13.05 on Thursday 21st September 2006. *Stephen Chapman*

BELOW: The importance of Bedlington as a key railway junction in this area cannot be overstated. Not least when one considers that stations are usually named after the places they serve but here, the community that grew up around the station is actually called Bedlington Station.

This view at Bedlington South is on Wednesday 24th August 1966. The crossing gates are open but the signal has yet to be pulled off for J27 No. 65815 waiting in the closed station with an Up coal train formed of 21 and 16-ton wagons. *Neville Stead collection*

LEFT: Bedlington South signal box on Monday 18th October 2004. *Stephen Chapman*

BELOW: Bedlington station looking north on Monday 1st August 1966 with K1 2-6-0 No. 62027 heading an Up coal train from the Morpeth direction. As at Seghill, colliery lines on the Down side meant that Bedlington had to make do with just one through platform on the Up side, though as can be seen there was also a north-facing bay here. In this case the apparently rusty track going left is to Bedlington "A" and Doctor pits, formerly of the Bedlington Coal Co., as well as to the Bedlington Brick Co. A Gresley full parcels brake sits in the bay platform.
Neville Stead collection

Goods facilities at Bedlington, situated on the Up side north of the station, were listed in 1956 as equipped for general goods, livestock, horse boxes and prize cattle vans and included a 1½-ton permanent crane. They were withdrawn with effect from 7th June 1965 but the station, closed to passengers since November 1964, continued to handle parcels until June 1966.

ABOVE: How the Bedlington scene had changed within 20 years. BR/Sulzer "Peak" Type 4 No. 45049 heads through the denuded but still extant station with the southbound "Blyth Spirit" railtour on Tuesday 27th August 1985. The station remains intact in 2016 and will hopefully see passengers again in the not too distant future. *Neville Stead*

RIGHT: The Blyth & Tyne remained a paradise of semaphore signalling well into the 21st century. This was Bedlington North on Monday 18th October 2004. The line to Morpeth veers left - and on this day showed little sign of use - while the line to Blyth and Lynemouth goes right of the box. *Stephen Chapman*

ABOVE: Choppington station, one mile and 636 yards north of Bedlington on the Morpeth line, closed to passengers when the regular service was withdrawn on 3rd April 1950 but was retained for special trains and parcels. On Saturday 21st September 1957 J21 0-6-0 No. 65110 arrives with a class B special. *Neville Stead collection*

The back of the train is passing the goods yard which consisted of two sidings on the Down side(left) and one on the Up side. In 1956 it was listed as able to handle all classes of freight except for carriages and motor cars. The crane, situated with a cattle dock on the Up side was able to lift up to 2½ tons. The yard also served an Esso petrol depot. West of the yard was the junction with a short branch going north to Choppington Colliery, beyond that, on the Down side, was Foggo's Siding serving the works of Choppington Wirecut Bricks, and then the junction with the branch going south to Netherton Colliery. At some point since this picture, the signal box was replaced by a modern structure on the opposite side of the line.

BELOW: NCB No.2 Area 0-6-0ST No. C18, Robert Stephenson & Hawthorns 7952 built in 1957, outside the engine shed at Choppington Low(or 'A') pit. From there a half-mile colliery line continued north to High(or 'B') Pit. No. 7952 was the last "Stubby Hawthorn" saddle tank built and one of the last steam locos built by Stephenson & Hawthorns. *Neville Stead collection*

The 264-yard single track to Choppington Colliery was known as the Low Pit Branch. It was operated according to One Engine in Steam regulations under the control of Choppington Station signal box with a maximum line speed of 15mph. It fell to the pit on a gradient of 1 in 213. Following closure of the colliery in 1966 the branch was deleted from the Sectional Appendix per an instruction issued 11th March 1972.

The single line to Netherton Colliery was 734 yards long and rose on a 1 in 347 gradient. It was also operated by One Engine in Steam under Choppington Station box with a 15mph maximum speed.

Netherton Colliery remained totally steam worked with Hunslet Austerity 0-6-0ST No. 47 (3166 of 1944) until closure in 1975. Barclay 0-4-0ST No. 50 (2245 of 1947) was spare loco until transferred to Shilbottle Colliery near Alnmouth.

As a result of colliery closures and subsequent singling of the line to Hepscott, Choppington Station box ceased to be a block post per a supplement dated 8th February 1975. The Netherton Colliery branch was not deleted from the Sectional Appendix until a supplement dated 6th March 1976, access being controlled by Netherton Colliery Ground Frame locked from Hepscott signal box in the interim.

NETHERTON COLLIERY BRANCH. The regulations for Working of Single Lines by One Engine in Steam apply between the Up stop signal, worked from Choppington signal box, and Netherton Colliery Sidings. Locomotives or trains, however, may be allowed to enter the line between Choppington and the Down stop signal for refuge purposes or for the purpose of working Messrs. Foggo's Brickyard Siding, while another locomotive in possession of the train staff is at Netherton Colliery sidings or standing at the Up stop signal.

A key is attached to the train staff for the gate leading on to the branch, and the driver will be held responsible for seeing that the gate is locked by the fireman after the locomotive and train have passed through in either direction. *BR NE Region Sectional Appendix 1960 and Eastern Region Sectional Appendix 1969.*

Hepscott station, just under a mile and a quarter from Morpeth, closed to passengers on 3rd April 1950 but, like Choppington, was retained for excursions and parcels. A 1950s excursion in the hands of G5 0-4-4T No. 67341 waits at the single platform.
The small goods yard on the left was equipped to handle general goods traffic only and had no permanent crane.
Both Hepscott and Choppington closed to goods on 9th March 1964.
Neville Stead collection

ABOVE: The Blyth & Tyne station buildings at Morpeth as they were on Monday 3rd March 2003. The goods shed at the far end was added when the terminus was converted into a goods station. *Stephen Chapman*

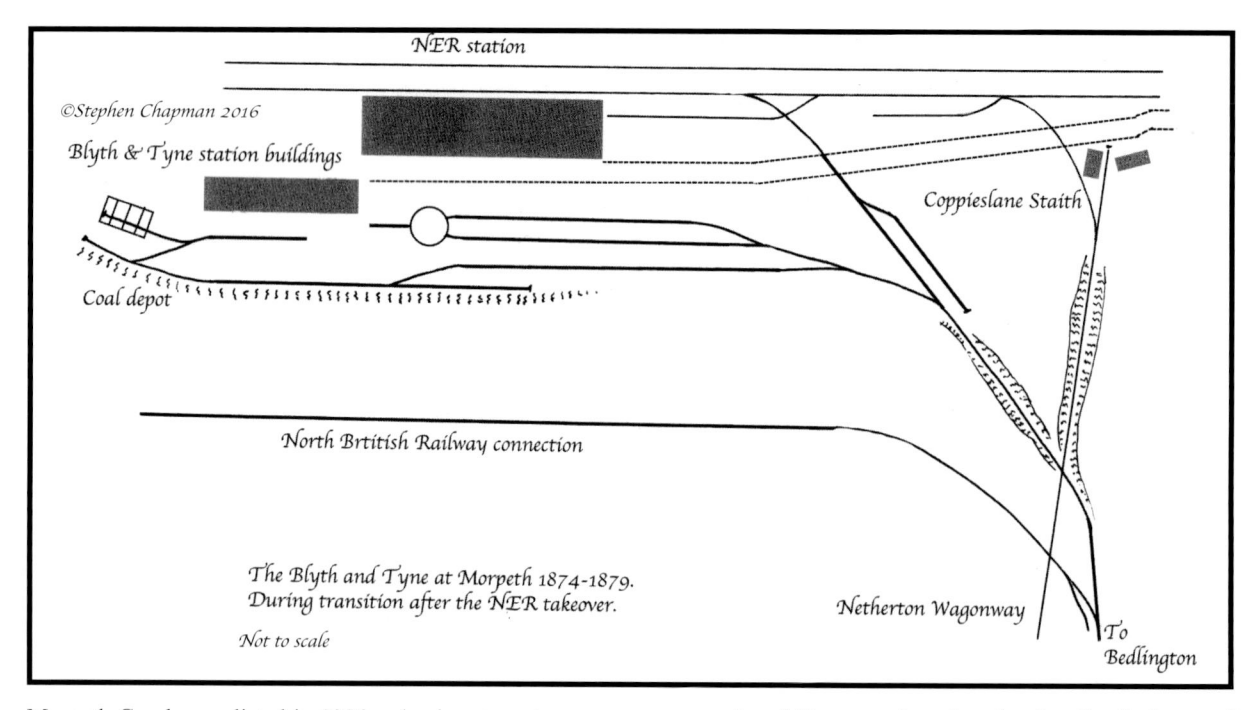

The Blyth and Tyne at Morpeth 1874-1879. During transition after the NER takeover. Not to scale

Morpeth Goods was listed in 1956 as having a maximum cranage capacity of 10 tons and equipped to handle all classes of freight. It remained in business until the 1980s.

OPPOSITE: The only timetabled class A express passenger service to use a substantial portion of the Blyth & Tyne. The summer Saturday Whitley Bay to Glasgow has reversed at Morpeth and is being taken forward by V2 2-6-2 No. 60807 in the early years of nationalisation. The bay platforms provided by the NER in 1880 for Blyth & Tyne services are on the left. *Neville Stead collection*

ABOVE: The nearest so far that there has been to a regular passenger service again on the Blyth & Tyne north of the Newcastle Metro despite a succession of proposals. This short portion at Morpeth is used for turning back units working stopping services over the East Coast main line from Newcastle. Empty Pacer No. 142071 awaits its return to Newcastle with the 14.50 departure on 3rd March 2003. In 2007 a feasibility study found that using the turnround time to extend this service to Bedlington would attract 60,000 - 85,000 passengers a year but nothing happened. In the foreground are the remains of the goods sidings following the route of the B&T into its original Morpeth terminus. *Stephen Chapman*

BEDLINGTON-NEWBIGGIN

ABOVE: Viewed from the Morpeth line at Bedlington North on Friday 20th September 1957, G5 No. 67281 starts a Newbiggin service out of Bedlington station which looks very smart having recently had a lick of paint. *Neville Stead collection*

BEDLINGTON TO NEWBIGGIN

British Railways North Eastern Region Sectional Appendix October 1960

Signalling: Absolute Block Bedlington-Woodhorn. Electric Token on single line Woodhorn-Newbiggin Station.

Maximum speed on main and single lines: 40mph

Signal Boxes: West Sleekburn(1600 yards from Bedlington North,) Marcheys House(989yds from West Sleekburn,) North Seaton Station(754yds;) Ashington Station(1 mile 154yds.,) Woodhorn(1 mile 123yds.,) Newbiggin(1 mile 412yds.)

Gradients: 1in 247 Ashington-Woodhorn

The 1969 Sectional Appendix showed no appreciable change except that following closure of the Woodhorn-Newbiggin section the BR line terminated at Woodhorn which was the junction with the NCB continuation to Lynemouth. Woodhorn signal box was abolished and North Seaton reduced to a gate cabin per a supplement issued on 11th March 1972. Woodhorn was replaced by the location(not a block post) Lynemouth Colliery NCB, 3 miles 228 yards from Ashington Station box. The line from Ashington to Lynemouth Colliery became shown as a goods line with no block signalling.
Signalling arrangements were further changed per a supplement issued on 8th February 1975. The route was then listed as Bedlington to Lynemouth Colliery(NCB.) It was shown as goods lines signalled by Absolute Block to Ashington Station and goods lines with no block from there to Lynemouth. West Sleekburn box had been abolished, the junction being worked by Bedlington North.

ABOVE: The English Electric Type 3s were the mainstay of Blyth & Tyne freight for many years after the end of steam until largely superseded by the more powerful Class 56s. No. 37058 passes Marcheys House Junction, a mile and a half north of Bedlington, with coals to Newcastle on Monday 12th December 1983. *Neville Stead*

BELOW: North of Bedlington the River Wansbeck is crossed by the second of the Blyth & Tyne's two impressive ironwork viaducts. Viewed from North Seaton in 1967, an unidentified J27 heads an Up freight, the first wagon of which states "House Coal Concentration." At the far end of the viaduct can just be seen on the left Marcheys House signal box and the signals for the junction to North Blyth, and beyond it the spoil tip for Bomarsund Colliery. The houses of Stakeford are just visible on the right.
Roger Holmes/Photos from the Fifties

ABOVE: Closed North Seaton station looking towards Ashington on 31st July 1966.
Neville Stead collection
North Seaton had a small goods yard which was equipped to handle general goods, livestock, horse boxes and prize cattle vans. It closed to goods on 9th December 1963.

LEFT: North Seaton signal box, abolished as a block post in 1972 but retained for control of the level crossing. This was how it looked on Wednesday 29th March 2006.
Stephen Chapman

A single track branch ran to North Seaton Colliery. Originally the last 490 yards of the North Seaton Colliery Co.'s line from Bedlington, it was worked according to "One Engine in Steam" rules with a maximum line speed of 15mph. The branch was abandoned after the colliery closed in 1961

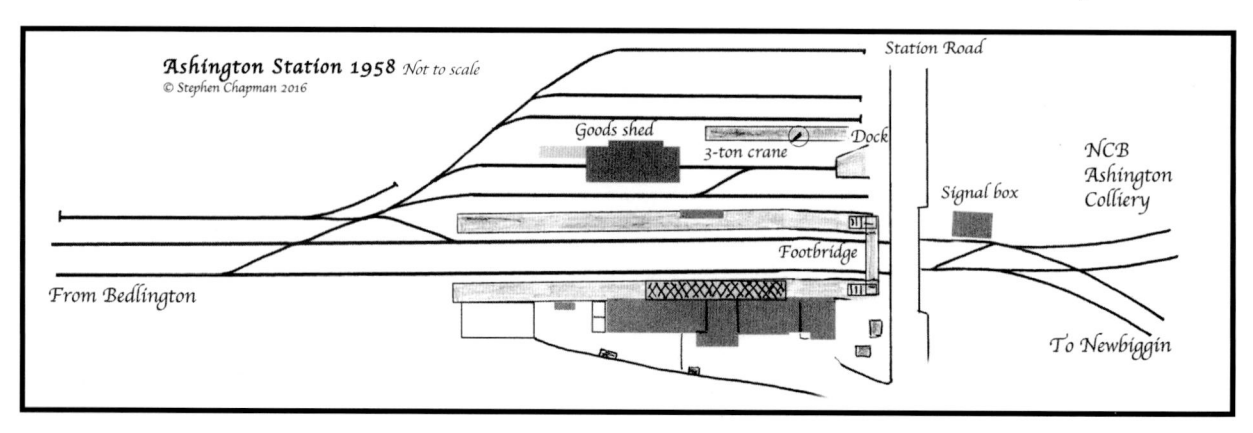

ABOVE: A supermarket carrier bag adorns Ashington signal box as 66157 approaches the station, where the platforms remained, with the 14.40 Lynemouth Alcan-Tees Yard aluminium ingots at 15.27 on Monday 12th September 2005. In the shadow on the left is the junction with the by then disused UK Coal line to Butterwell via New Moor and Potland. *Stephen Chapman*

BELOW: J27 No. 65789 passes the NCB engine shed at Ashington Colliery while starting out with a load of 21-ton hopper wagons. *Neville Stead collection*

ABOVE: BR Type 5 No. 56126 gets an MGR coal train on the move from Ashington Colliery on Tuesday 23rd September 1986.

BELOW: Hirst Lane level crossing on the BR line from Ashington to Woodhorn is visible in the left background as ex-BR class 14 Paxman diesel hydraulic 0-6-0 NCB No. 506(formerly BR No. D9504) turns away from the BR line and heads towards New Moor with coal from Lynemouth on Saturday 7th June 1986. The BR line towards Ashington goes out of the picture to the right and is denoted only by the home signal showing above the NCB train's brake van. Above that can be seen the headgear of Woodhorn Colliery while on the far left of the horizon is Lynemouth power station. Compare this view with that on page 18 to see how much the area changed over the ensuing 20 years. *Both Neville Stead*

ABOVE: Just over two miles 500 yards from Ashington came Newbiggin-by-the-Sea: pit village-cum-fishing village-cum-seaside resort-cum-haunt of artist L. S Lowrey, and the end of the line so far as the Blyth & Tyne was concerned, although there was originally a plan to continue north to Warkworth. This view looking out of the station shows G5 0-4-4T No. 67277 after arrival with an incoming service on Friday 5th August 1955. The mop and bucket in the foreground and open carriage doors suggest the cleaners are either about to start of have just completed their work. Newbiggin Colliery can be seen in the left background but notice also the neat garden.

BELOW: In this scene looking towards the end of the line, V1 2-6-2T No. 67645 awaits its headlamp prior to leaving the well kept station with a service to Manors on the same day. At this time the goods yard on the right was listed as able to deal with all classes of freight except for carriages and motor cars so there was no vehicle dock. The permanent crane, just partly visible on the loading dock on the extreme right, could lift up to one ton. Newbiggin closed to passengers and goods on 2nd November 1964. *Both Neville Stead colln.*

55

NORTH AND SOUTH BLYTH

ABOVE: Winning Junction is where the curves from Marcheys House to the north and West Sleekburn to the south meet and form the Cambois Branch to North Blyth. J27 No. 65861 takes the Marcheys House curve with empty hopper wagons destined for Ashington on Tuesday 2nd August 1966. *Neville Stead collection*

LEFT: Winning signal box and the booms protecting the level crossing with the Stakeford to East Sleekburn road instead of gates or barriers. Monday 16th October 2006. *Stephen Chapman*

CAMBOIS BRANCH (GOODS LINE)

British Railways North Eastern Region Sectional Appendix October 1960

Signalling: Absolute Block(Permissive Block on Up line Winning to West Sleekburn.)

Maximum speed on main lines: 35mph

Signal Boxes: Winning(844 yards from West Sleekburn,) Freeman's(1626 yards from Winning,) Cambois(1336 yards,) North Blyth(1517 yards.)

Gradients: 1in 104(falling) West Sleekburn-Winning

The 860 yard curve to Marcheys House was signalled by Absolute Block with a 20 mph maximum speed.

The 1969 Sectional Appendix showed the branch terminating at North Blyth Ground Frame in place of the signal box. One Train Working was introduced between Cambois and North Blyth per an instruction issued on 17th November 1973 with the note: "Trains must travel to North Blyth on the Arrival line and return on the Departure line." Cambois signal box was reduced to a gate cabin only and One Train Working extended back to Freemans per a supplement issued on 8th February 1975.

BELOW: At Freeman's Crossing was the junction with the lines into Blyth Cambois power station and the signal is "off" for J27 No. 65811 and its coal train to enter the "A Group" sidings from the Winning direction. Q6 0-8-0 No. 63362 and brake van on the back end appear to be hitching a ride rather than assisting as they dropped off here and continued to North Blyth after 65811 and its train had cleared the junction. "A" was the older of the two power stations having opened in 1960. *Brian Connell/Photos from the Fifties*

At "A" power station drivers of BR trains were instructed to detach their wagons in the Reception Sidings or as otherwise directed by the CEGB(power station) hopper controller and then depart with empty wagons. Loaded wagons would be taken to the discharge hoppers by a CEGB locomotive.

ABOVE: At the later Blyth Cambois "B" power station, which came fully on stream in 1966, the rail operation was more like an early form of merry-go-round system whereby the locomotive stayed with the train and hauled it through the discharge hoppers before departing with the same train for another load. Trains first had to pass over an electronic weighbridge no faster than 6mph. If the wagon buffers were not kept apart from each other false weigh readings could accumulate and then the whole process would have to be done again. After weighing and removal to the reception sidings the engine ran round the train before hauling it through the discharge hoppers. Unlike MGR, the train would stop, six wagons at a time over the hoppers, to discharge. Movements were controlled by a series of special signals showing various white and red aspects informing the driver whether to stop immediately, to move forward at slow speed, or to reverse at slow speed. After discharge the train was hauled, again at 6mph, over another weighbridge while a carriage & wagon examiner checked for any defective wagons. If there were any, they would be left in the cripple siding. With the well stocked cripple siding on the right and the discharge control signals on the left, English Electric Type 3 No. 37074 approaches the power station with coal from Ellington in October 1985, shortly before conversion to full MGR working. *Malcom Roughley*

BELOW: At Cambois the short branch to West Blyth staiths left the line to North Blyth. Here, begrimed and rusting J27 No. 65879 threads its way along the staiths branch on Saturday 19th June 1965 with a load of coal for shipping. *R. Patterson/Colour-Rail*

ABOVE: Looking the opposite way from the minor road bridge from which the previous picture was taken, J27 No. 65815 awaits its next move at the approach to West Blyth Staiths. Across the fields in the background are the extensive power station sidings.
David Lawrence/Photos from the Fifties

BELOW: The chimneys of Blyth Cambois "A" and "B" power stations were a prominent landmark visible from a long distance. This scene in October 1985 shows BR Type 5 No. 56097 heaving empty MGR hoppers out of the West Blyth staiths empty sidings and under the minor road leading from Cambois to the power station site perimeter. The two sidings in the foreground are part of Cambois diesel traction depot. *Malcolm Roughley/Stephen Chapman archive*

59

ABOVE: J27 No. 65847 waits for the signal to clear at the entrance to the West Blyth staiths loaded sidings while an unidentified K1 2-6-0 and brake van await their next move. The North Side Staiths ground frame from which points and signals were locally controlled is in the building to the right of the K1 and just beyond the brake van kip on the lower level. *Brian Connell/Photos from the Fifties*

BELOW: A more recent view but now also a long time ago. Class 08s work simultaneously shunting HAA merry-go-round hoppers on Friday 15th July 1988. On the left No. 08666 pushes loaded wagons towards West Blyth staiths while 08421 deals with the empties on the lower level. As can be seen, other traffic besides shipping coal was handled in these sidings. The giant gantry in the background is part of the power station ash disposal system. *Neville Stead*

ABOVE: The vast length of West Blyth staiths is emphasized by this picture when one considers that the camera lens cannot accommodate the whole structure. The date is December 1989, no ships are present and the staiths are about to close. *Stephen Chapman*

BELOW: Class 08 shunter No. 08747 pushes MGR hoppers along West Blyth staiths way above the collier *Jylland* berthed alongside. Much of the coal leaving the staiths went to such northern European countries as Denmark as well as to power stations on the Thames. The immensity of the timber structure had to be seen to be believed - timber was far more suitable than iron or steel as it was both lighter and not subject to salt water corrosion. *Colour-Rail*

ABOVE: On the deck of West Blyth staiths looking south in October 1985. The trackwork is of particular interest, especially one of the scissors crossovers which allowed the movement of wagons to and from the various spouts without having to move all the other wagons on the staiths. In the misty distance on the right a Class 56 and MGR train can just be made out at Bates Colliery, on the south bank.

LEFT: A view towards the end of the staith with one of the coal spouts in the foreground.
Both Malcolm Roughley/Stephen Chapman archive

A supplement to the 1972 BR Eastern Region Sectional Appendix issued on 6th March 1976 stated that Class 17 and 37 locomotives were allowed on to West Blyth staiths, in emergencies only. Is it conceivable that the only two surviving Class 17s, at the Derby Research Centre, might find their way to the staiths?

ABOVE: The end of West Blyth staiths, beyond which is a long drop into the waters of Blyth harbour.

BELOW: The view looking inland at wharf level as the Glasgow-registered *Peacock Venture* is loaded by conveyor with coal for Ireland. The berth for loading barges with power station ash is on the right. *Both Malcolm Roughley/Stephen Chapman archive*

Local historian George Tuff was one of the last teemers employed on West Blyth staiths when the final shipment of coal left on 31st December 1989.

A teemer for 43 years, he recounted the following to the Bellcode publisher just before the staiths closed: "We must have been the last manual teemers in England and definitely on BR because everything is now mechanised plant. We're a very old trade, older than the railway itself. Teemers were loading coal from the Plessey wagonway onto the river in the 1700s.

"Before the end of the 17th century the harbour consisted only of the natural river channel, except for small quays or landing places built to handle coal and salt, the latter from salt pans at the upper part of the river. There was insufficient depth of water to load a full cargo so boats known as "keels" were used. By 1730 a coaling quay, a ballast quay, a pilot's watch house and a lighthouse had been constructed, and in 1765 the first breakwater had been built on the rocks east of the channel. The first staiths with an elevated loading point were built in 1788. The base of one of these can still be seen on the south side as part of a building housing a blacksmith's shop. The first wooden staith to be built, on the south side of the river, was by the Blyth & Tyne Junction Railway in 1849; coal shipment grew to 200,000 tons a year.

"Of the seven teemers left most have worked at least 20 years on the staiths. We worked in "corps" of four men, working together for years until one was promoted to trimmer, working on the ships.

"Teemers were a race apart for although they were railwaymen, graded latterly as senior railmen, they had their own pay and conditions, even their own rule book.

"To the day we finished we were paid by an ancient system called "keelage." It was based on the old 18th Century keel boats and we were paid according to each keel loaded - equal to 21 1/2 tons. If you worked hard you could earn good money. There was a myth that teemers were the richest men in Blyth.

"Some coal was easier and quicker to load than others which had a direct bearing on your pay packet. We got the best money loading pond duff, washed smalls or slack, which had the consistency of wet cement. Right to the last we preferred Widdrington opencast which was very free flowing. We'd say Shilbottle Best came ready-wrapped because it was mined from between layers of white pyrites so it had a white coating. It was good house coal and we shipped special loads for Buckingham Palace.

"The teemers work on the staiths about 70ft above low water, on a platform 45 to 50ft wide and half a mile long, with open water on three sides and below, exposed to the elements all year round.

"One man 'rides on,' that is to say he marshalls the pilot engine and the coal it shoves up on to the staiths, then gravitates the wagons, eight at a time down to the teeming point where the "chock man" stops the wagons with a wooden chock and then, using a chock and a 6lb mallet, chocks the wagons door by door on to the hopper. And with 6,000 tons loaded in HAA wagons, that entails 216 wagons - 648 doors!

"The next man 'knocks in,' that is he knocks off the safety catches and opens the bottom doors of the wagons as they come on to the hopper. He also operates the conveyors that carry the coal out over and into the ship.

"The fourth man is called the "trapper," the name comes from the days when spouts or gravity chutes were used to load ships. The trapper controlled the flow of coal down the spout, now he gravitates the empty wagons off the staiths. Both he and the 'rider on' walk miles whilst loading is taking place. The coal shipping foreman was in overall charge .

"At one time there were 74 of us on BR working two shifts. About 24 men worked on the NCB side, now down to six or eight. The last of a breed of hundreds on the North East coast."

Seen from Cambois signal box, J27 No. 65815 heads towards North Blyth with a brake van in the spring of 1965. Another J27 can be seen on the line to West Blyth staiths. Within a couple of years, the open ground between them will have become Cambois diesel depot. In the distance, beyond the signals, are Cambois Colliery sidings while two coal trains can just be made out through the haze queueing for access to the staiths.

David Lawrence/Photos from the Fifties

Cambois diesel depot was opened in 1967 to replace the two steam sheds at North and South Blyth. Despite supplying the locomotives for a busy self-contained freight network it never had its own allocation, not even shunters, using instead locomotives out-stationed from Gateshead where they returned for heavy maintenance. Following sectorisation of British Rail in the 1980s, Cambois became the responsibility of the Trainload Coal sub-sector whose locomotives were allocated to Toton, near Nottingham. Maintenance facilities at Cambois were thus upgraded so that more work could be done there instead of returning locomotives all the way to Toton. It also achieved BS5750 quality assurance accreditation. But by then the coal industry was under attack with pits closing, exports declining and traffic haemmoraging away. With all but one pit closed and the last staiths closing at the end of 1989, what traffic remained could be handled by locomotives sent from Tyne Yard and Cambois depot closed in 1996.

ABOVE: This view shows the south end of the shed in October 1985 with Class 56 and 37 locomotives present.
Malcolm Roughley/Stephen Chapman archive

BELOW: This view from the same minor road as illustrated on page 59 shows the sad state of the closed depot on Monday 18th October 2004. Facilities added since the above picture include an extra lean-to covered area over the road on which the Class 56 above is standing, and at this end of the shed a heavy lift hoist. Also in the picture is the boarded up admin building and, in the foreground, the disused line to the by then demolished West Blyth staiths. *Stephen Chapman*

ABOVE: A view of Cambois depot in happier times on Friday 15th July 1988 from the same vantage point as the previous picture, by which time the lean-to shed had been added. A fine selection of wagons is on display. *Neville Stead*

BELOW: Looking north at North Blyth, dirty and rusty J27 0-6-0 No. 65802 heads loaded 21-ton hoppers towards the staiths on Saturday 19th June 1965. The Cambois Colliery Railway and the North Sea are on the right. *R. Patterson/Colour-Rail*

ABOVE: Looking south at North Blyth with J27 No. 65789 alongside the signal box on Tuesday 2nd August 1966. Dock and shipyard cranes on the south side reach up above the engine; out of the picture to the right is the long-established shipbreaking yard of Hughes Bolckow while the sidings leading to North Blyth staiths can be glimpsed between the brake van and the signal box. On the left is the NCB's Cambois Colliery railway going towards its own NCB and Cowpen staiths. The line to the Alcan alumina import berth now follows this route and is the only railway remaining here in 2016 along with a connection to the Battleship Wharf coal import terminal, established in the area on the right in 2006. *Neville Stead collection*

BELOW: A product of rebuilding at York Queen Street locomotive works, as denoted by its rounded cab, J77 0-6-0T No. 68427 shunts North Blyth sidings on Friday 20th April 1956. By 1959 the J77s had been replaced by 204hp diesel shunters. Four of these and 350hp shunter No. D3679 were allocated to the Blyth sheds until 1962. After that diesel shunters were supplied by Percy Main until that shed closed upon which they were supplied by Gateshead. *Colour-Rail*

67

ABOVE: Hughes Bolckow were shipbreakers but their yard will be better known to readers of this book as one of the places around the country where many BR steam locomotives were cut up, including a good many favourites. One of those favourites, A4 Pacific No. 60024 *Kingfisher* awaits its doom. The yard had closed by 1982. *Neville Stead*

BELOW: North Blyth loco yard as seen from the higher vantage point of the staiths sidings on Friday 12th December 1952. Motive power on display consists of the usual J27 0-6-0s and J77 0-6-0Ts. The coal stage and water tank are prominent while wagons can be seen on the Cambois Colliery line and staiths sidings in the distance. *Colour-Rail*

Along with its sister at South Blyth, North Blyth shed was coded 52F in the British Railways era but they were two independent depots. North Blyth shed was a roundhouse and provided purely goods engines for the endless procession of coal trains which ran on former Blyth & Tyne metals as well as tank engines for work on the staiths and local shunting. North and South Blyth were among the last steam depots in the North East and finally closed in September 1967 when Cambois diesel depot was opened and steam abolished. This scene inside North Blyth roundhouse on Saturday 2nd October 1954 shows engines ranged round the turntable. From left they are: J27s Nos. 65877 and 65811, J77s Nos. 68397, 68427 and 68399, and J27 No. 65786. These were engines built specifically for the job that needed doing in these parts; there was even a street nearby named after their designer. Consequently, the depot allocation, for the most part but not always, lacked variety. However, towards the end, as the ageing J27's were gradually withdrawn and replaced by "newer" classes, the allocation became a little more varied, as seen below. Other engines carrying the 52F shedcode since the 1950s included Ivatt Class 4 2-6-0s, B1 4-6-0s, Q6 0-8-0s, J39 0-6-0s, J25 0-6-0s and BR Standard Class 3 2-6-0s. *Neville Stead collection*

LOCOMOTIVES ALLOCATED TO NORTH BLYTH SUMMER 1950: J27 0-6-0: 65783/6/9/97/9/801/4/11/9/28/51/67/70/6/7/79/80/92. J77 0-6-0T: 68397/8/405/17/26/7. Total: 24

LOCOMOTIVES ALLOCATED TO NORTH AND SOUTH BLYTH NOVEMBER 1966: Ivatt class 4MT 2-6-0: 43000/12/40/8/55/63/71/97/101/23/32/3/7/8; B1 4-6-0: 61014 *Oribi/* 61386; K1 2-6-0: 62005/11/7/24/7/57/9/60/2/7; J27 0-6-0: 65795/804/11/2/3/5/23/34/8/42/55/60/1/2/9/79/82/92. Total: 44

On 24th February 1963, Alex Scott noted the following at North and South Blyth: Q6 0-8-0: 63352/6/9/81/ 86/3429; J27 0-6-0: 65792/4/65801/8/10/9/20/2/8/34/55/7/61/75/9/80/9/90/1/3. BR/Gardner 204hp 0-6-0: D2105/ 66. Total: 28

PRIVATE SIDINGS AT BLYTH, 1956

North Blyth: Cambois Colliery and Cowpen shipping staith; Hughes, Bolckow Shipbreaking Ltd.; British Iron & Steel Corporation Salvage Ltd. (via Hughes Bolckow Siding.)

Blyth[South]: Blyth Dock & Shipbuilding Co.; Cowpen Quay Depots, King Street Siding; Mollers Stores Ltd.(via Blyth Dock & Shipbuilding Co. siding;) NCB Bates Colliery and shipping staith; NCB Cowpen "A" Pit; NCB Cowpen Crofton Mill Pit; Star Foundry Co.(via Blyth Dock & Shipbuilding;) Blyth Harbour Commissioners' Estate.

Blyth Harbour Commissioners' Estate: Atkinson, Glover, Burnip & Co.; Gatheral Timber Import Co.; P. Grayston & Co.; South Harbour and Import Dock; T. Stephenson & Sons; G. & N. Wright Ltd.

ABOVE: The coaling stage at North Blyth with the roundhouse in the background and J27 No. 65879 receiving a top-up. This is the north end of the shed, looking south. *Neville Stead collection*

BELOW: In 1962/63 the Blyth sheds received a considerable influx of Q6 0-8-0s from Blaydon. Here in 1963, No. 63429, still bearing its 52C Blaydon shedplate, is seen in company with another classic, a 1950s Hillman Minx, outside the south end of the roundhouse, by the entrance just off Worsdell Avenue. Behind it is another incomer from Blaydon, No. 63402. *Arthur Chester*

ABOVE: The Ivatt Class 4 2-6-0s were among late transfers to the Blyth sheds and altogether 18 members of the class passed through the allocation between 1965 and the end of steam, most ending their days there. Additional to these was No. 43140, a former Scottish and then Stainmore line engine, seen here with J27 No. 65869. It was at 52F from November 1964 until June 1965. Also, 43126 was allocated there for a month before being moved on to York in September 1961. *Colour-Rail*

BELOW: J27s Nos. 65789 and 65880 rest in the yard at North Blyth motive power depot at 2.5pm on Sunday 25th March 1962. A particular point of interest in this scene is the rudimentary signal on the Cambois Colliery Railway which runs by on the other side of the fence. *Robert Anderson*

ABOVE: After the "High Ferry", a vital chain-drawn vehicle ferry linking the North and South Blyth communities folded, and with no government support forthcoming for its retention, the Blyth Harbour Commissioners provided a replacement service for pedestrians only using their own harbour launches. Here we see ferry No. 5 about to dock at North Blyth with Bates Colliery across the water behind it. On the extreme right is the NCB's Bates coal shipping wharf. *Arthur Chester*

BELOW: The view of North Blyth staiths from the approaching ferry on Wednesday 15th August 1968. In charge of 21-ton hoppers is BR Class 03 204hp 0-6-0 diesel No. D2056, one of the replacements for the erstwhile J77s. Behind the staiths are rows of terraced houses provided by the NER for its workers. *Adrian Booth*

The North Blyth Staiths branch was a goods line consisting of two sections operated according to One Engine in Steam regulations. The first section which could be occupied by one train was from Summit to the north end of No.8 Spout. The second section which could be occupied by one train ran from No.1 Spout to Summit. No.1 Spout and Summit were shown in the BR North Eastern Region Sectional Appendix as a Block Post. The maximum speed allowed was 15 mph. The 1969 Sectional Appendix showed the same arrangement. The branch was deleted from the Sectional Appendix per a supplement issued on 8th February 1975.

ABOVE: Although a sight still to be witnessed at the time of publication, this picture is well worthy of inclusion. The line on which 66183 is arriving at the Alcan alumina import terminal at 15.25 on Monday 18th October 2004 is the route of the Cambois Colliery railway. It ran to its own Cowpen(so-called because it was owned by the Cowpen Coal Co. before nationalisation) and NCB staiths. *Stephen Chapman*

BELOW: On to the south side of the river. At the Blyth platform of Newsham station, G5 0-4-4T No. 67281 blows off impatiently while the crew are absorbed in something of interest in the early evening paper on Friday 20th September 1957. *Neville Stead collection*

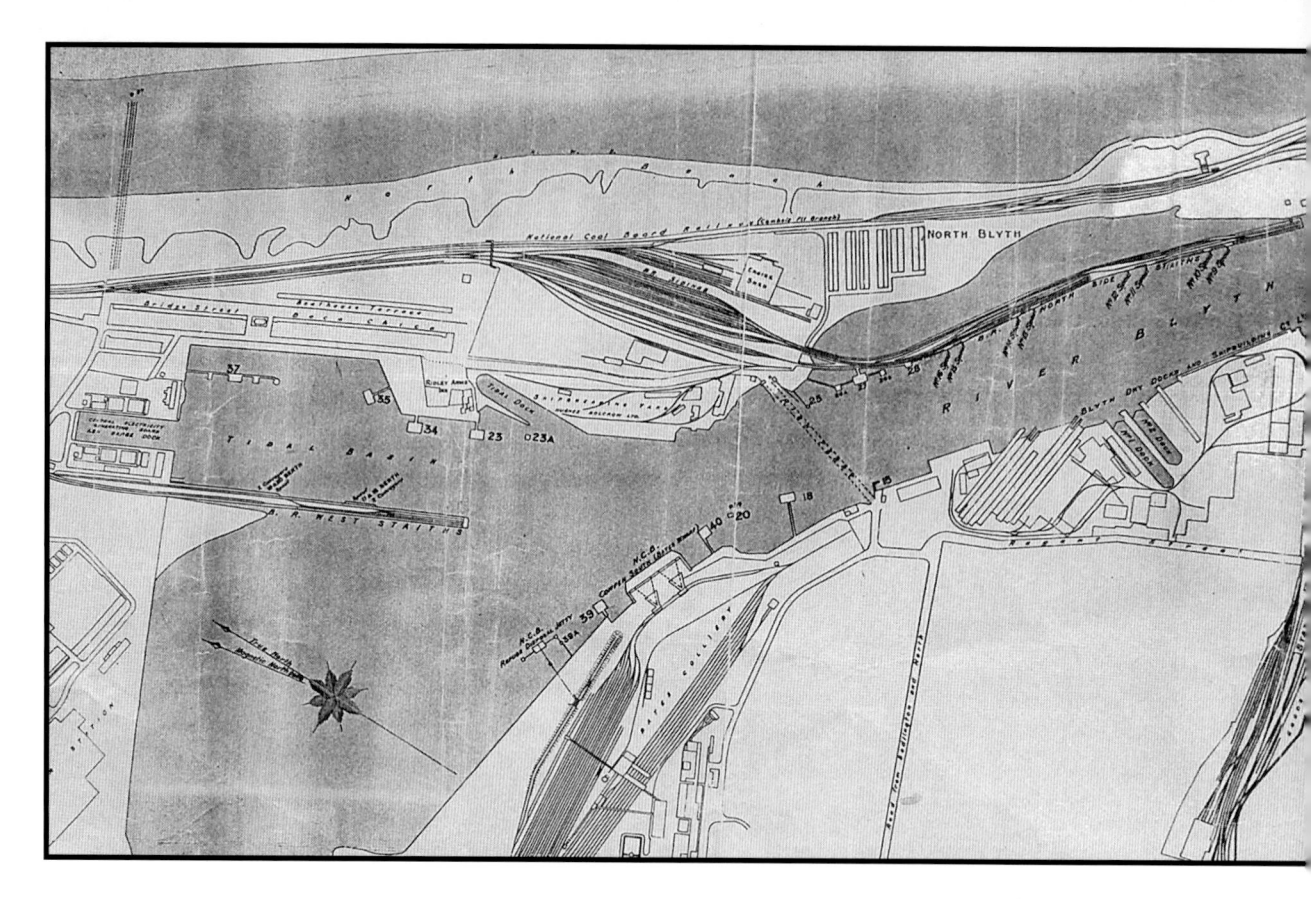

ABOVE: This 1950s Blyth Harbour Commissioners map shows the extent of the railway, colliery, staiths and harbour lines at Blyth during that era. In 2015 only one line to the alumina import terminal at the very end of the peninsular on the north side remains along with a siding serving the coal import terminal on the site of the shipbreakers' yard.

BELOW: J27 No. 65819 waits in the Blyth sidings at Newsham with a train of empty 21-ton hopper wagons on Monday 1st August 1966. The chimneys of Cambois power station reach for the sky on the distant horizon. *Neville Stead collection*

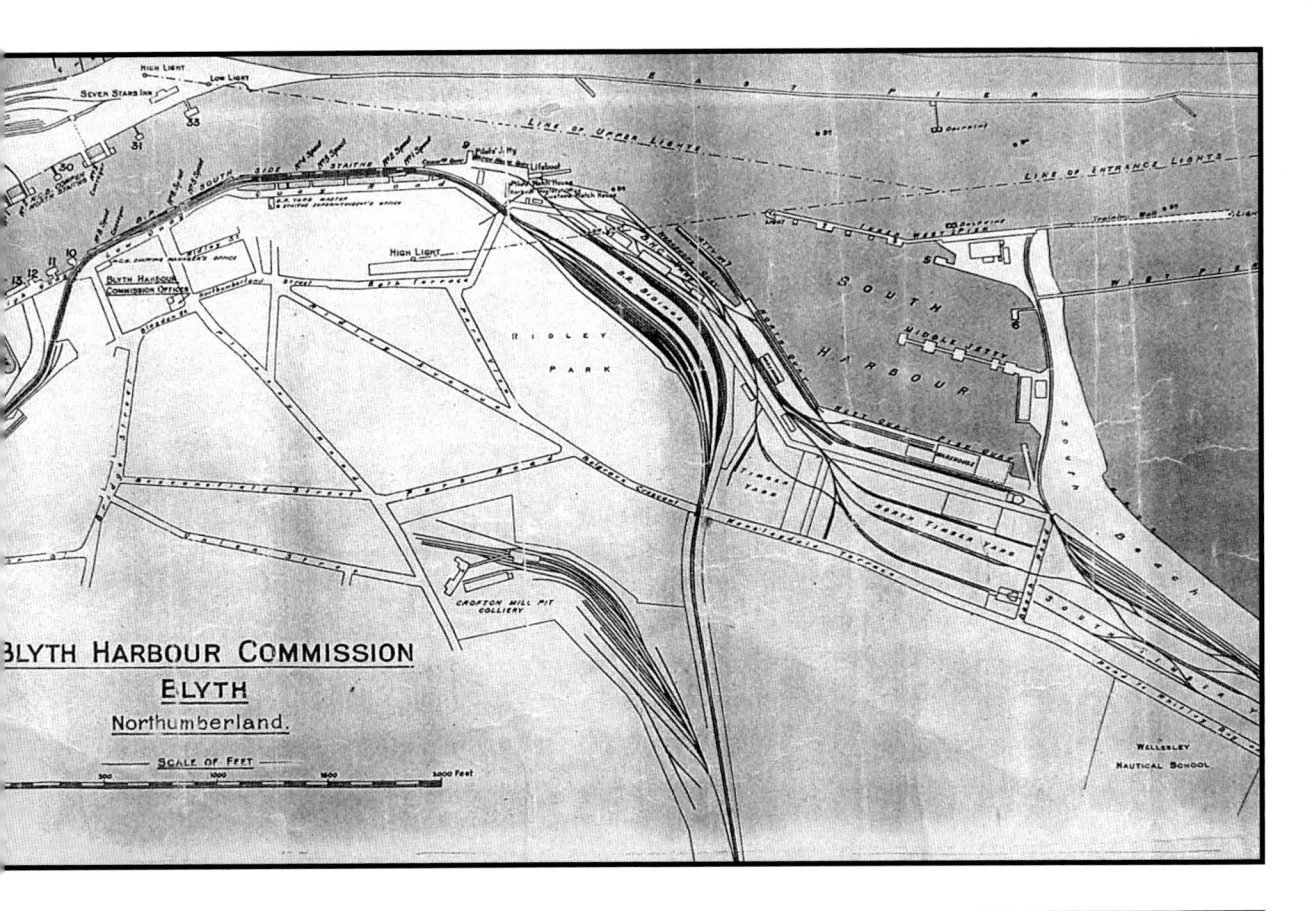

RIGHT: Heralding the approach to Blyth station from Newsham was the level crossing with Cowpen Road. Blyth Crossing signal box, seen here on Saturday 17th May 1958, was just a gate cabin until Blyth signal box was destroyed by a world war two air raid in 1941, after which it was equipped to control all of Blyth station, approaches and sidings.
Beyond this crossing was another where an NCB line went to Isabella via Cowpen 'A' Pit(closed 1935.) South Blyth engine shed is on the far right.
Neville Stead collection.

Newsham North Junction to Blyth station was shown in the British Railways North Eastern Region 1960 Sectional Appendix as signalled by Absolute Block with signal boxes at Isabella(499 yards from Newsham North,) and Blyth(1 mile 346 yards from Isabella. The maximum line speed was 45mph.
The 1969 Sectional Appendix showed the branch downgraded to a single goods line operated according to One Engine in Steam regulations between Isabella and Blyth Links Road via the South staiths and harbour area. It was subsequently closed and deleted from the Sectional Appendix per a supplement issued on 11th March 1972.

South Blyth shed was, like North Blyth, coded 52F by British Railways and for many years it was difficult for the observer to tell which engines belonged to which depot. However, South Blyth had one vital difference to North Blyth in that it was a mixed depot providing engines for passenger services as well as freight and so had an allocation of passenger and mixed traffic engines besides the usual J27s. At one time, South Blyth also provided an engine outstationed at Reedsmouth on the former North British line from Morpeth. Most of its passenger fleet consisted of the G5 0-4-4 tanks which operated the push-pull services to Monkseaton and Newbiggin together with some J21 0-6-0s. South Blyth also differed from North Blyth in that it was a six-road straight shed with an outdoor turntable.

ABOVE: J77 0-6-0T No. 68431 and G5 No. 67277 give the impression that they are pulling a rake of wagons from the NCB line but in fact they are just parked on a siding in this 1950s scene.

BELOW: Inside the shed with J27s Nos. 65862 and 65893. *Both Neville Stead collection*

LOCOMOTIVES ALLOCATED TO SOUTH BLYTH, SUMMER 1950

J21 0-6-0: 65080; G5 0-4-4T: 67244/6/61/95/326/34/41/7.   J27 0-6-0: 65781/80/10/24/9/34; J77 0-6-0T: 68424/8/31. Outstationed at Reedsmouth: J21 0-6-0: 65035. G5 0-4-4T: 67296.   Total: 20

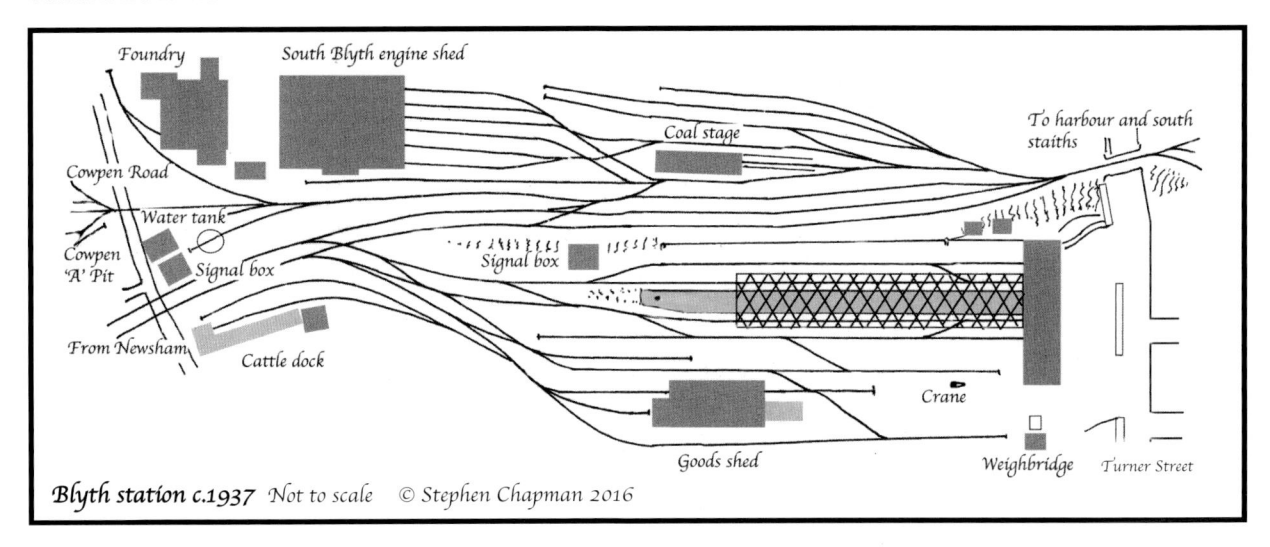

Blyth station c.1937   Not to scale   © Stephen Chapman 2016

BELOW: G5 No. 67311 sits in steam outside the shed on Saturday 17th May 1958. Its days numbered, 67311 was withdrawn in November when passenger services were turned over to diesel multiple units. *Neville Stead collection*

ABOVE: There are features worthy of note by modellers in this scene of J27s 65834(left) and 65821 simmering quietly among the piles of ash outside South Blyth shed. The clock on the gable end above 65834's dome is so coated with grime that it and the time of 12.25 are barely visible while on the right the wagon is loaded with ash which, of course, had to be removed from all steam depots, often for re-use as track ballast. *Neville Stead collection*

BELOW: The allocation of the last J21 0-6-0, the now preserved No. 65033, to South Blyth for the last year of her working life on BR until April 1962 is well known but she was no stranger there, nor was the class in general. J21s, often a pair at a time had long carried the 52F shedcode, one out-based at Reedsmouth. No. 65033 had been allocated to South Blyth at various times at least since 1955. During 1960, she was there with 65070 which was withdrawn that September. *Peter Rose*

ABOVE: Seen from the engine shed area on 20th September 1952, G5 No. 67261 propels a 'Rail Motor' service into Blyth station.

BELOW: Many of the railway features around Blyth station are on view in this scene looking east, also on 20th September 1952. A G5 0-4-4T is hauling a passenger service out of the station, the carriage siding and goods depot are on the right, the coaling stage for the engine shed on the far left, and the lines to the harbour and the South Staiths continue left of centre. The signal box destroyed by bombing was situated between the harbour lines and the passenger train. *Both Neville Stead collection*

79

ABOVE: This undated 1950s view is looking out from the station and shows the fine canopy with G5 No. 67323 in the platform. The lines to the harbour are higher up on the right where the tank wagons are. *Neville Stead collection*

BLYTH STATION[Crossing] SIGNAL BOX RULE 96. Before a train is allowed to enter an already occupied platform line it must be brought nearly to a stand at the Down Home signal, which may then be lowered and a green hand signal exhibited from the signal box. After this has been acknowledged by the driver giving a short whistle, the signal giving access to the particular platform line may be lowered.
If the green hand signal is not acknowledged in this manner, the train must be brought to a stand at the signal giving access to the platform, before that signal is lowered, and a driver must understand in such circumstances that the platform line concerned is partially occupied and must proceed cautiously only as far as the line is clear. *No. 2 Supplement to the LNER General and North Eastern Operating Area Sectional Appendices 1947, issued by BR, March 1958, and North Eastern Region Sectional Appendix 1960.*

BELOW: Looking towards the buffer stops at Blyth station on Saturday 13th October 1962 with a Metro-Cammell DMU occupying one of the platform lines and the goods yard crane on the right. *Chris Gammell/Photos from the Fifties*

ABOVE: Departmental vehicles and the goods depot are on the left, G5 No. 67340 occupies the near platform, another G5 is on coaching stock in the opposite platform, and hopper wagons are on the harbour line. *Neville Stead collection*
Blyth was listed in 1956 as able to handle all classes of goods while the permanent crane could lift up to 10 tons. Blyth station goods yard and depot were closed with effect from 23rd September 1963 although goods traffic continued to be handled at private sidings around the area.

BELOW: The desolate scene deep within the station shortly before closure with a Metro-Cammell DMU present on Friday 1st May 1964.
Ray Oakley/Colour-Rail

ABOVE: J27 No. 65812 shunts at Crofton Mill Colliery in June 1965. On the embankment to the right is the line from Newsham to Blyth station via South Blyth Staiths. *Colour-Rail*

NEWSHAM-BLYTH VIA STAITHS double track goods line was signalled by Absolute Block on both lines between Blyth and Crofton Mill and on the Down line between Crofton Mill and Isabella. Permissive Block was in force on the Up line between Crofton Mill and Isabella. The maximum line speed was 15mph. Signal boxes were at Links Road(1 mile 221 yards from Blyth station,) Crofton Mill(743 yards from Links Road,) and Isabella(1429 yards from Crofton Mill.) *BR North Eastern Region Sectional Appendix 1960.*

Movements onto and off South Blyth Staiths were controlled by the use of two separate train staffs, one each for the single line between the notice board at the south end of No.1 Spout and the notice board near the Coal Shipping Foreman's office, and for the single line between the notice board near the Coal Shipping Foreman's office and the notice board west of No.8 Spout. The Coal Shipping Foreman was in charge of all train staff working. The train staffs were kept in the guard's room and receptacles were also provided for them near No.1 Spout and west of No.8 Spout. Should an engine require to leave the staiths to work Crofton Mill, the gas works siding, or for loco duties, and then return to the staiths, the train staff had to be placed by the fireman or guard in the guard's room receptacle, or with the permission of the Coal Shipping Foreman, in the receptacle near No.1 Spout or West of No.8 Spout. Crofton Mill Colliery, worked by the Mickley Coal Co. from 1928 until nationalisation, closed in 1969 after which the section from Isabella to Links Road was also closed.

PREVIOUS PAGE BOTTOM: A 1970s scene at Bates Colliery with ex-BR Class 08 No. D3088 in NCB guise and bearing the legend "North East Area 2100/526." D3088 was scrapped on site in October 1985.
The collier *Landguard Point* is at the colliery wharf while beyond can be seen the silos of the Alcan alumina import terminal at North Blyth. *Neville Stead*

The 1960 BR North Eastern Region Sectional Appendix listed the BR single line to the NCB exchange sidings at Isabella Colliery as 192 yards long from the junction with the Blyth branch at Isabella signal box. It was worked according to One Engine in Steam rules and had a maximum line speed of 15mph. The 1969 Sectional Appendix showed the line as being 692 yards long from Newsham North, Isabella box having ceased to be a block post, the location being removed completely from the Sectional Appendix per a supplement issued on 8th February 1975. Bates Colliery and staiths closed in 1986 and all the line from Newsham with it, the last railway into Blyth.

RIGHT: In 1989/90 the whole disused line from Newsham to Bates was taken over by the British Coal Opencast Executive and completely rebuilt to carry British Rail MGR trains to a new deep water coal shipping terminal at Bates.
On Monday 8th April 1991 BR Type 5 No. 56127 returns from Bates along the former Bates-Isabella section with the empty wagons from the first train to supply the new terminal. The dominance of Cambois power station chimneys over the area is clearly apparent. Both the railway and power station are now gone. *Stephen Chapman*

EARSDON JUNCTION - PERCY MAIN

EARSDON JUNCTION TO TYNE COMMISSION QUAY

British Railways Eastern Region(Northern Area) 1969 Sectional Appendix

Signalling: Absolute Block on both lines Percy Main North-Tyne Commissioners'[TIC] No.1 signal box. Absolute Block on the Up Main and Permissive Block(Goods line) on the Down Main Earsdon Junction-Percy Main North

Maximum speed on main lines: 30mph(15mph on Tyne Commissioners' railway)

Signal Boxes: Blue Bell(590yds from Earsdon,) Percy Main North(2 miles 1319yds.,) Engine Shed(838yds,) TIC No.1(958yds,) TIC No.6(237yds,) TIC No.10(423yds,) TIC No.2(603yds.)

From Earsdon, the propelling of three wagons without a brake van to the Co-operative Siding at Blue Bell was permitted, according to a supplement issued in March 1958.

ABOVE: Having just passed under the A1058 Coast Road at Murton Row, J27 No. 65789 is seen between West Chirton and Middle Engine in 1967 with a heavy coal train assisted at the rear by 65879. On the right is the branch to Rising Sun Colliery while on the left, the NCB Backworth Railway climbs on the embankment ready to cross over the Blyth & Tyne about a quarter of a mile ahead of the train at High Flatworth. As the train is loaded, it has almost certainly originated at Rising Sun Colliery and is being directed to a destination further north, such as Blyth. Freight trains could be assisted in the rear on the Rising Sun branch as well as from Percy Main North to Blue Bell. This scene would not last much longer, apart from steam ending before the year was out, Rising Sun Colliery closed in 1969 and the branch to it was deleted from the Sectional Appendix per a supplement issued on 11th March 1972. *Neville Stead*

BELOW: The Percy Main section of the Blyth & Tyne was on its last legs by the time Sulzer Type 2s Nos. 25189 and 25236 called with The Venerable Bede railtour. The special is just about to pass under the A1058 Coast Road between Percy Main and Blue Bell. The course of the Backworth Railway is on the left. *Neville Stead collection*

ABOVE: Viewed from Wallsend Road, V1 2-6-2T No. 67646 approaches Percy Main North Junction with a boat train for Tyne Commission Quay. It will have to run round its train here before heading round the curve on the right. It has descended from Percy Main Station Junction on the Newcastle-North Shields electric line which is heading left to right on the horizon, and under which can be seen in the left background a line of NCB wagons on the Backworth Railway. In the centre background are the buildings of the original Blyth & Tyne station, closed to passengers as long ago as 1864, and the goods depot which lasted until April 1968. The Seaton Burn Wagonway used to run behind the first fence on the left. *Neville Stead collection*

BELOW: Percy Main engine shed looking north from the Howdon Road bridge. The building on the right is the old Blyth & Tyne Railway works, later used as a wagon repair shop and by this time as part of the motive power depot. The running shed, devoid of roof, is just visible behind the signal gantry. The Hartley Main railway is on the left. As was always the case, J27s are wandering about like feral cats. *Neville Stead collection*

In the BR era, Percy Main was coded 52E and was dedicated to providing engines for mineral traffic. Consequently, its allocation consisted almost entirely of J27 0-6-0s. The depot comprised a double ended running shed with three through roads and a single road into an adjoining building at the north end. The old Blyth & Tyne works building had two dead end roads plus three more in a later addition built on the west side. Although renowned for its J27s, Percy Main also had a substantial allocation of diesel shunters from 1963 - including those previously allocated to the Blyth sheds - which it supplied to locations across Tyneside and the Blyth & Tyne. The depot closed to steam in February 1965 and completely in February 1966.

ABOVE: A selection of J27s led by 65795 on the left, stands in the roofless through shed on Sunday 25th March 1962. On the left hand road can be seen a shelter which was erected to protect shed staff from the elements after the roof had been removed. *Robert Anderson*

BELOW: J27s fill the running shed on 6th June 1948 when it still had a roof. They include 5821, 5852 and 5796. *T.B. Owen/Colour-Rail*

LOCOMOTIVES ALLOCATED TO PERCY MAIN JUNE 1955: J27 0-6-0: 65780/4/91/5/6/9/802/6/7/9/12/3/4/21/5/6/31/7/9/42/52/8. Total: 22   *In the 1950s, breakdown crane No. 901636 was based at Percy Main.*

SUMMER 1963: Q6 0-8-0: 63394; J27 0-6-0: 65790/1/5/6/802/5/9/12/3/4/21/5/31/42/58/60/9; BR/Gardner 204hp 0-6-0: D2044/5/7/8/9/50/5/92/3/2104/5/6/65/6/310/1/2/3/5/21/2/6/7/8/9/32/3/4/5/9; Drewry 204hp 0-6-0: D2249; 350hp 0-6-0: D3078/242/3/4/322/4/ 673/4/8/9/938/9/42. Total: 62

ABOVE: It wasn't all coal on the Blyth & Tyne as witnessed by this view of J27 No. 65861 shunting general goods stock in Engine Shed Junction Sidings alongside Engine Shed signal box at Percy Main. The picture is undated but it is clearly towards the end of steam as so much of the railway here has been removed, including track on the coal stage(left.) Compare this scene with that on page 1. The sidings being shunted led to Seghill Staiths in Northumberland Dock that were abandoned by the 1940s. The empty space in the foreground used to be occupied by the Hartley Main's East Howdon sidings which led to its own staith. The staith survives in 2015 having been incorporated into a Tarmac aggregate depot. Engine Shed was the last BR box before the TIC system. *Roger Holmes/Photos from the Fifties*

PERCY MAIN BOOKED FREIGHTS 1960 - all class H

Time	Days	Working
2am	MX	Percy Main-Heaton Up Yard Returns Heaton North-North Shields
Untimed	MX	2-3.30am Heaton North Yard-Percy Main No.2
		Return working of the 1am Earsdon-Heaton
6am		Percy Main-Walker
Untimed		after 10.15am Heaton North Yard-Albert Edward Dock
		Worked by engine and men off 6am Percy Main-Walker
4.10pm		Percy Main-Heaton Up Yard
4.45pm	SO	Percy Main-Heaton Up Yard
Untimed	SO	5.30-6.25pm Heaton North Yard-Percy Main No. 2
		Return working of 4.45pm from Percy Main
Untimed		after 6.40pm Heaton North Yard-Percy Main
		Worked by engine and men off 5pm Tynemouth-Forth
Untimed	SX	after 9.20pm Heaton North Yard-Percy Main No. 2
		Worked by engine and men off 5pm Willington Quay-Low Fell
Untimed	SX	after 10pm Heaton North Yard-Percy Main Station Yard
		Return working of 6pm Walker-Heaton

The 1969 BR Eastern Region Sectional Appendix stated that unfitted trains proceeding to Engine Shed Junction Sidings should be halted at Percy Main North for wagon brakes to be applied before descending the gradient and the wagon brakes not released until its destination. Trains heading towards TIC No. 6 signal box must be halted at Engine Shed Junction for wagon brakes to be applied and not released until reaching Albert Edward Dock or Whitehill Point. According to a supplement issued on 8th February 1975 these instructions were changed to read only that trains proceeding to Northumberland or Albert Edward docks should stop at Percy Main North for wagon brakes to be applied and not released until reaching Whitehill Point or Albert Edward Dock.

The early 1970s saw progressive rationalisation between Percy Main North and the various riverside locations which included the closure of Engine Shed signal box at Percy Main and Tyne Commission Quay passenger station(both deleted from the Sectional Appendix per a supplement issued on 17th November 1973) and radical simplification of the track layout south of Percy Main North. Also, TIC No. 1 signal box had closed by 1972. By the this time just a single goods line operated under One Train Working rules went from Percy Main North to the Port of Tyne Authority(formerly the TIC,) and a separate single goods line from Percy Main North to an Esso oil terminal which occupied most of the former railway around Engine Shed Junction. This was also operated according to One Train Working rules. A ground frame controlled all movements in and out of the Esso terminal under supervision of the Esso Sidings Supervisor. Two trains could enter the sidings provided the driver of the first train handed the single line Train Staff to the Sidings Supervisor for returning to the signalman at Percy Main North.

The southern extremity of the Blyth & Tyne. These two pictures taken on 25th October 1952 show staiths at Northumberland Dock. Those below, at least, appear to be disused, the sunken boat adding an air of dereliction but through the timberwork a ship can just be discerned at the next set of staiths. Through the haze, across the river, can be seen Tyne Dock and the huge iron ore hopper where the trains to Consett would soon be loaded. In the picture above a tramp steamer sails by on the Tyne(right).
Of particular note in both pictures is the sharp gradient down onto the spouts - did any wagons ever end up going off the end into the dock? Northumberland Dock has since been partially filled in and landscaped to create a wetlands nature reserve while the remainder is disused and silted up. *Both Neville Stead collection.*

ABOVE: Deep within the TIC system, J27 No. 65795 has just passed TIC No. 9 signal box on its way from Whitehill Point with empty coal hoppers. On its way back to BR, it will pass No. 6 signal box and then No.1 signal box before reaching the BR box at Engine Shed Junction. No. 9 box, which can be seen left of the back of the train, was abolished during the 1960s. The track on the far right serves a timber stacking ground while that diverging left is the connection down from the Backworth Railway which is on the embankment.
Both pictures on this page: Roger Holmes/Photos from the Fifties.

BELOW: J27 No. 65861 on general trip duty passes TIC No. 8 signal box while en-route to Percy Main from the Albert Edward Dock sidings that were situated on the east flank of the TIC engine shed which can just be seen through 65861's exhaust, beyond the telegraph poles. The train is just about to pass under the Backworth Railway on the approach to TIC No. 6 box. The line to Nos. 9 and 2 boxes, the south west side of Albert Edward Dock and Tyne Commission Quay curves away right. On the left is the TIC engineers' depot.

ABOVE: At the extremity of BR workings over the TIC railway was Tyne Commission Quay, situated on a peninsular at the south east corner of, and on the outside of, Albert Edward Dock. It consisted of two wharves for passenger ferries, the Bergen Wharf facing the Tyne, and the Oslo Wharf facing the dock entrance. V3 2-6-2T No. 67691 is seen waiting at the Bergen Wharf platform with with a King's Cross boat train. *C. P. Gordon Stuart/Colour-Rail*

BELOW: The TIC had a sizeable fleet of its own shunting engines which were, in the main, rather elderly. Standing by the engine shed is 0-6-0ST No. 11, built by Robert Stephenson & Co. at their Forth Banks, Newcastle, works in 1901, works No. 3072. The van on the higher level is lettered "T.I.C. LOCO TOOL VAN." *Neville Stead collection*

ABOVE: With a ship and dockyard cranes forming the backdrop, veteran TIC 0-6-0ST No. 2 shunts at Albert Edward Dock. No. 2 dates from 1875 and was built in Gateshead by Black, Hawthorn & Co., works No. 337. *Neville Stead collection*

BELOW: The end of the line at Percy Main. It is almost impossible to imagine that this is the same place as in the picture on page 92. All that remains is this track serving the Esso oil terminal established in the late 1960s where trains were loaded as well as emptied. The lines to the TIC railway and Albert Edward Dock have all been lifted whilst Engine Shed signal box has given way to a squat ground frame cabin. It is Tuesday 7th June 1983 and even what little remains is about to close as Type 3 No. 37045 prepares to haul tanks away. The terminal had three sidings; No.1 for loading inflammable black oil; No. 2 for loading highly flammable white oil; and No. 3 for spare tanks and discharge of inward loaded tanks. Esso hired a Class 08 from BR to shunt the depot. In the background, across the river, are the tanks of the Jarrow terminal which still receives a daily train in 2016. *Neville Stead*

THE COLLIERY RAILWAYS

ABOVE: This gloriously antiquated scene on the Hartley Main Collieries railway at Percy Main shows double-framed 0-6-0 No. 3 storming out of East Howdon sidings and past the LNER's Engine Shed signal box with returning empties. No. 3 is ex-NER Class 93 No. 658 built by Robert Stephenson & Co. in 1867. When scrapped in 1959 it was the oldest NCB locomotive in Northumberland.

BELOW: Out on the double track main line of the Hartley Main system, 0-6-0ST No. 24 heads north with empties near High Flatworth Farm while a loaded train for Percy Main complete with brake van passes in the other direction. Judging by the absence of a van on 24's train, it will not be traversing the LNER. No. 24 was one of a considerable number of Barry Railway Class F 0-6-0STs disposed of by the Great Western Railway and sold to North East collieries. As GWR No. 724, it was acquired by the Hartley Main company in 1933 where it stayed until the system closed in 1960 when it was scrapped. *Above: E.E. Smith/Neville Stead colln. Below: Neville Stead colln.*

ABOVE: At the same location as the previous picture but after nationalisation had taken place in 1947, 0-6-2T NCB No. 27 heads a northbound train of empties complete with brake van this time. No. 27 was also ex-Great Western, that company's No. 154, and was acquired by Hartley Main in 1934. It was built in Leeds by Kitson & Co. in 1908.

BELOW: At Seghill the Hartley Main parted company with the Blyth & Tyne and went west to Dudley and north to East Cramlington, hence its original name, the Cramlington Railway. In the colliery sidings at East Cramlington on Thursday 16th June 1953 was NCB 0-6-2T No. 28, formerly Great Western Railway No. 227 and previously of the Barry Railway. *Both Neville Stead collection*

TOP: Another Hartley Main ex-Great Western locomotive. This one is at West Moor, Killingworth, on Friday 4th September 1953 where the pit had closed in the 1930s but sidings and a loco shed remained into the 1950s. Built by Beyer Peacock, No. 29 was originally on the Rhondda & Swansea Bay Railway, becoming No. 802 when that company was absorbed by the GWR in 1922.

CENTRE: Also at West Moor, on Tuesday 3rd June 1952, NCB 0-6-0ST No. 21 *Skiddaw Lodge.* This engine originated with the Cleator & Workington Junction Railway and became LMS 11568 before joining the Hartley Main.

BELOW: A more "modern" view on the branch to Dudley Colliery. In 1968, NCB Robert Stephenson & Hawthorns 0-6-0ST No. 59, built in 1954, works No. 7802, takes water from the torpedo-shaped tank so typical of colliery systems.
All Neville Stead collection

ABOVE: At Seaton Delaval Colliery was the main depot and works of the Hartley Main system which Hartley Main trains travelled over the Blyth & Tyne from Seghill to reach. Back in the 1950s an utterly fascinating array of industrial and former main line locomotives of considerable historic value could be found there. From left, the engines outside the workshops on Friday 4th September 1953 were ex-NER 93 class 0-6-0 No. 3, Robert Stephenson & Hawthorns 0-6-0STs Nos. 42 and 41, and 0-6-0T No. 29. *Neville Stead collection.*

BELOW: Few engines at Seaton Delaval could be more fascinating than this - the elegant and enigmatic Hartley Main No. 20, in absolutely sparkling condition following overhaul in early NCB days. No. 20 originated with the Glasgow & South Western Railway and passed into LMS ownership as No. 17196. Following withdrawal, 17196 was sold to the Kirkheaton Colliery Company in 1926 to become the only locomotive on the short-lived Wallridge Mineral Railway which ran over the Northumberland fells from Darras Hall to Belsay Colliery. When that closed in 1930 she languished unused until 1942 when she was called up for war service by the Board of Trade and used at Cambois opencast mine. After the war, she went to Backworth and in 1949 to Seaton Delaval, being scrapped in 1953, alas many years before any hope of preservation. As No. 20, she replaced an ex-Great Northern Railway 0-6-0 scrapped in 1946. *N. Stead colln.*

LEFT: Hartley Main No.12, pictured here at Seaton Delaval, is ex-NER 0-6-0ST No. 313. The picture is undated but withdrawal and scrapping in 1935 appear imminent.
This engine has a long history, starting as a 2-4-0 built by Kitson & Co. of Leeds in 1847, being rebuilt in its present form as NER 287 class in 1878.
Neville Stead collection

RIGHT: The USA 0-6-0 tanks weren't just confined to the Southern Region of BR. This example, built by Davenport in 1943, works No. 2509, is NCB No. 35, seen at Seaton Delaval on Sunday 3rd May 1953.
Neville Stead collection

LEFT: The colliery railway system was even used for distributing the wages on payday. This old Cramlington Coal Company pay carriage is seen at Seaton Delaval on Monday 14th September 1953.
Neville Stead collection

ABOVE: Seaton Delaval Colliery and sidings looking east on Friday 4th September 1953. The structure on the right is the original pit, sunk in 1838.

RIGHT: This machine seen in Seaton Delaval workshop was top secret and so photographs of it are rare. It is an experimental giro-electric locomotive built by Sentinel with Swiss equipment in 1957, works No. 9614.
The flywheel was "re-charged" by the probes in front of the cab striking poles along the lineside. *Both Neville Stead collection*

COLLIERIES IN THE BLYTH & TYNE AREA 1956 (main line connection in brackets)

NCB Northumberland & Cumberland Division No.1 Area (South Northumberland)

Algernon(Holywell)
Blue Bell Brickworks (Holywell)
Burradon(Killingworth)
Eccles(Holywell)
Fenwick(Holywell)
Havannah(Killingworth)
Hazlerigg(Killingworth)
Maude(Holywell)
Rising Sun(Percy Main)
Weetslade(Killingworth)

No.2 Area (Central Northumberland)
Bates(Blyth)
Bates shipping staiths(Blyth)
Bedlington "A"(Bedlington)
Bedlington Doctor(Bedlington)
Bomarsund "F"(Bedlington)
Cambois(North Blyth)
Cambois shipping staiths(N. Blyth)
Choppington Low(Choppington)
Cowpen "A" Depot(Blyth)
Crofton Mill Depot(Blyth)
Cowpen Isabella(Newsham)
Cramlington Brickworks and Lamb Pit(Annitsford)
Dinnington(Killingworth)

Dinnington Brickworks
Dudley(Annitsford)
Hartley(Hartley)
Horton Grange(Bebside)
Howdon staiths(Percy Main)
Howard Pit(Choppington)
Netherton Hall(Choppington)
New Delaval(Seaton Delaval)
Newsham(Hannah Sdg)
North Seaton(N. Seaton)
Seaton Burn(Killingworth)
Seaton Delaval (Seaton Delaval)
Seghill(Seghill)
Seghill Brickworks(Seghill)

Shankhouse(Annitsford)
West Sleekburn "E"(N. Seaton)

No.3 Area (North Northumberland)
Ashington(Ashington)
Bothel Park or Ashington Jn. Sdg.(Ashington)
Coneygarth Sdg.(Ashington)
Ellington(Ashington)
Linton(Ashington)
Lynemouth(Ashington)
Newbiggin(Newbiggin)
Potland Sdg.(Ashington)
West Moor Sdg(Ashington)
Woodhorn(Ashington)

97

ABOVE: On the Backworth Railway, NCB Austerity 0-6-0ST No. 4, built by Robert Stephenson & Hawthorns in 1944, works No. 7166, hauls empties away from the Backworth staiths at Whitehill Point in March 1967. *Roger Holmes/Photos from the Fifties*

BELOW: Progressing further and having just passed over the TIC Railway, NCB No. 4 heads north alongside the Howdon Road-Tyne Commission Quay road while returning the empties to Backworth. *Roger Holmes/Photos from the Fifties*

ABOVE: In typical British summer weather on Monday 1st August 1966 the flagman halts traffic on the B1322 for NCB 0-6-0T No. 39(Hudswell, Clarke 1824) to cross. Apart from a length extending behind the photographer retained as a shunting neck, the whole line south of this point to Percy Main was closed in 1969. A new connection installed in 1975 removed the need to shunt over the road.

BELOW: Just by the first wagon in the above picture, the one-time East Holywell Coal Company's branch struck off right, crossed the B&T on the level and went to Fenwick Colliery about a mile away. In this view Robert Stephenson & Hawthorns 0-6-0ST No. 24 marshalls NCB internal wagons at Fenwick Pit. *Both Neville Stead collection*

99

ABOVE: At Fenwick Pit with Robert Stephenson & Hawthorns 0-6-0ST No. 16(works No. 7944 of 1957) shunting the screens.
Both pictures on this page Neville Stead collection

BELOW: Continuing straight ahead from the B1322 crossing, the Backworth Railway came to Eccles Colliery where this glorious sight could be encountered. This was the engine shed for the whole system which as late as 1972, after closure of the line to Percy Main, still required five locomotives in use on weekdays. The 0-6-0STs pictured from left are: Austerity No. 48(Hunslet 2864 of 1943,) No. 16, and Austerities Nos. 49(Stephenson & Hawthorns 7098 of 1943) and 6(Bagnall 2749 of 1944.) Nos. 48 and 16 are on the line which continued to Backworth 'C' pit.

A collection of ex-main line veterans in the yard at Eccles Colliery during the early 1950s.
TOP: Pannier tanks were no strangers to the colliery railways of the North East. NCB No. 7 seen here used to be No. 714 on the Great Western Railway before joining the Backworth Railway.
Originally a Barry Railway 0-6-0ST No. 714 came to the Backworth Coal Co. in 1934. When withdrawn in 1956 the boiler, tanks and wheels were used to rebuild ex-GWR No. 719 which worked on at Rising Sun Colliery until 1962.

CENTRE: This is NCB 0-6-0ST No.1(Robert Stephenson 1664 of 1875) which came from the NER where it was No. 1357.

BOTTOM: A rather cleaner NCB No. 2(Robert Stephenson 1671 of 1876) but scrapped in 1954, seen here on Tuesday 19th June 1951. It had at one time been on the NER as No. 1364.
All Neville Stead collection

101

ABOVE: At the north end of Eccles Colliery at Church Road level crossing, and on the line connecting the colliery to the Burradon & Holywell Wagonway, Austerity 0-6-0ST No. 49 assists a departing train of loaded BR hoppers on Friday 25th June 1971. *Adrian Booth*

BELOW: On the Burradon & Holywell, a Robert Stephenson & Hawthorns 0-6-0ST climbs towards the 200ft contour and away from a crossing with the B1322, mid-way between Backworth and Burradon, while working a westbound morning trip from Seghill which had run round at Holywell. *Neville Stead collection.* Although an NCB line, BR trains also used the B&H and it was listed in the BR Sectional Appendix, being described as signalled by electric token between Fisher Lane and Hazlerigg signal boxes.

ABOVE: Burradon was a colliery railway junction of some note, being where lines from Holywell, Coxlodge via Dinnington and Weetslade collieries, and from Killingworth, met the Seaton Burn Wagonway. Apart from a colliery there was also an engine shed, workshop and extensive sidings. In this view, Robert Stephenson & Hawthorns 0-6-0ST No. 42(works No. 7759 of 1953) helps Austerity 0-6-0ST No. 9(RSH 7097 of 1943) with a rake of BR hoppers at Burradon on 16th August 1968. Diesels would soon take over and by 1972 No. 9 was the only steam loco still in use at Burradon. The pit closed in November 1975 and the loco shed, replaced by a new shed at Weetslade in January 1976, was then only used as a store for preserved and surplus locomotives.

BELOW: On a test run after overhaul, Backworth's "Stubby Hawthorn" 0-6-0ST No. 16 (Robert Stephenson & Hawthorns 7944 of 1957) crosses the old A1 at Wideopen, on the former Seaton Burn Wagonway on Wednesday 18th October 1972. *Neville Stead collection*

Adrian Booth recalls the events that led to him capturing the above scene using his father's Zeiss Ikon folding bellows camera.

"A workman at the loco shed told me that Burradon's coal was tripped two miles west to Weetslade Washery. After washing, it was brought back for distribution.

"I heard the distant sound of a hard working steam locomotive and, storming up from Weetslade came RSH7802. Cars were stopped at the small level crossing as it stormed up the gradient, leaving a tremendous exhaust hanging in the clear blue sky. Shortly after, RSH7759 came pounding up in almost identical fashion. I walked beside the engine up to the top of the yard where it left its wagons and then backed down to the shed.

"RSH7097, the ninth RSH loco I'd seen at Burradon, came up the gradient from Weetslade with a very long train. It made an incredible sight and sound as the smoke rose high into the air, but it got into trouble on the bank, and its exhaust beats became slower and slower. No. 7097 then stalled, its rake of wagons blocking the road. One of the crew ran across to the shed and RSH7759 was quickly backed down to give assistance. The two engines, brewed up full steam, gave a mighty heave, and then blackened the sky as they slowly brought the train up and past me into the colliery yard."

103

TOP: Resting out in the fields and drizzle, possibly at West Moor, the Seaton Burn Coal Company's former Great Western 0-6-0ST No. 815. Built by Robert Stephenson & Co., it had originated with the Port Talbot Docks & Railway Co.

CENTRE: Basking in rural sunshine this time, Backworth shed's Robert Stephenson & Hawthorns 0-6-0ST No. 44 (works No. 7760 of 1953) sits at Havannah Colliery on 4th July 1973. This was on a branch off the former Coxlodge & Hazlerigg Collieries railway and by this time the western extremity of the colliery lines from Burradon until it too closed in November 1976.

BOTTOM: From Seaton Burn Colliery a mile-long main and tail rope-worked 2ft 6 in gauge line continued north west to Brenkley Drift Mine, adding yet more interest to the already fascinating network of colliery railways in this part of Northumberland. The train seen here on the approach to Brenkley is loaded with general materials rather than coal. Brenkley coal was washed at Weetslade but when that closed in 1981 it was taken to Ashington by road. Brenkley Drift and its narrow gauge line lasted until October 1985.

104

RIGHT: The entrance to the drift at Brenkley with narrow gauge line and conveyor descending underground side by side. The opening date of 1953 is proclaimed on the stone above the arch.
An array of notices warn of dire consequences should anyone dare to breach safety rules. On the left one states: "No person to ride material set." The large notice right of the arch states: "Any person found leaving the manriding set before it stops will be instantly dismissed."

CENTRE: The Cowpen Coal Company's No.11 at Cambois Colliery, North Blyth. This ex-London Brighton & South Coast Railway 0-6-0T had been acquired from the Southern Railway where it was No. 2143.

BELOW: There were so many ex-main line engines on the colliery railways hereabouts that they were like another main line system - but with more variety. At the Ashington Coal Company's engine shed No. 22, ex-Great Western 0-6-0PT No. 718, was keeping company with Hawthorn Leslie 0-6-0T No. 13(3392 of 1919.) *All pictures on pages 104 and 105: Neville Stead colln.*

105

Yet more ex-main line engines at Ashington. TOP: NCB No. 2 looking smart outside the workshops in June 1952 was an ex-Glasgow & South Western Railway 0-6-2T. It was acquired by the Ashington Coal Co. from the LMS where it was No. 16908.

CENTRE: One wouldn't expect to find a Great Eastern Railway loco in the North East any more than Great Western engines, but Ashington Coal Co. 0-6-0T No. 18 was LNER Class J66 No. 7275 in her past life,

BOTTOM: Ashington Coal Co. 0-6-0T No. 4, a London, Brighton & South Coast engine, came from the Southern Railway as No. B163. She is seen in the coal company's passenger station at Hirst on Wednesday 20th October 1937. *All Neville Stead collection*

ABOVE: Until 1966 the Ashington Railway boasted a regular passenger service for miners which ran between Ashington, Linton and Ellington. This was no ordinary "Paddy train" operation with converted wagons or vans but one using ex-main line coaching stock, mainly NER but one at least from the Furness Railway, and proper station platforms. This is the Ashington terminus at Hirst with coaching stock in both platforms. *Neville Stead collection*

BELOW: An Ellington-Ashington NCB miners' train passes Linton with a Robert Stephenson & Hawthorns 0-6-0ST in charge. Linton signal box and colliery are in the background. *Neville Stead collection*

ASHINGTON COLLIERY RAILWAY: The National Coal Board Ashington Colliery Railway is worked in accordance with the BR Permissive Block Regulations for Goods lines. At all signal boxes on the colliery railway, a green hand signal held steadily will be exhibited to the driver of a freight train if the section is occupied by another freight train and if this signal is acknowledged by the driver, the signal controlling the entrance to the section will be lowered.
BR Eastern Region(Northern Area) Sectional Appendix 1969

ABOVE: The end of steam is approaching, both on BR and on the NCB at Ashington, but Ashington loco shed and works were still well stocked with genuine industrials on Saturday 10th June 1967. The engines being besieged by a party of gricers include, from left: Austerity 0-6-0ST No. 47, with its bunker to the camera another Austerity, Robert Stephenson & Hawthorns 0-6-0ST No. 41, Peckett 0-6-0ST No. 6(2023 of 1941) with an Austerity and another RSH 0-6-0ST behind it, Austerity No. 27 and in the right background another RSH 0-6-0ST. Ashington engine shed closed when internal rail operations ceased in March 1987. *Neville Stead collection*

BELOW: Such a large steam fleet needed all the servicing facilities of a main line depot. Here, Peckett 0-6-0ST No. 6 stands by the loco coal stage which is being fed by BR hopper wagons, suggesting that loco coal was brought from elsewhere.
Roger Holmes/Photos from the Fifties

ABOVE: With the workshops on the right, Austerity 0-6-0ST No. 51(built by Bagnall of Stafford in 1944, works No. 2757) goes about its business shunting BR 21-ton hoppers in the sidings at Ashington Pit in 1967. *Roger Holmes/Photos from the Fifties*

BELOW: No. D9511, the first of the 650hp Class 14 Paxman diesel hydraulic 0-6-0s to be acquired by the NCB from British Rail arrived at Ashington in January 1969 with another ten following over the next 23 months, plus three more from within the coal industry by 1975(a total of five also went to Burradon.) By 1972 Robert Stephenson & Hawthorns 0-6-0STs Nos. 41 and 43 were the only steam locomotives left at Ashington, both of them stored out of use. This is class prototype D9500(NCB North East Area No.1) dealing with loaded internal wagons at Hirst Steps on Tuesday 8th October 1985. Ashington Colliery dominates the background and New Moor stocking site is away to the right. Ashington Pit closed in March 1988. *Neville Stead*

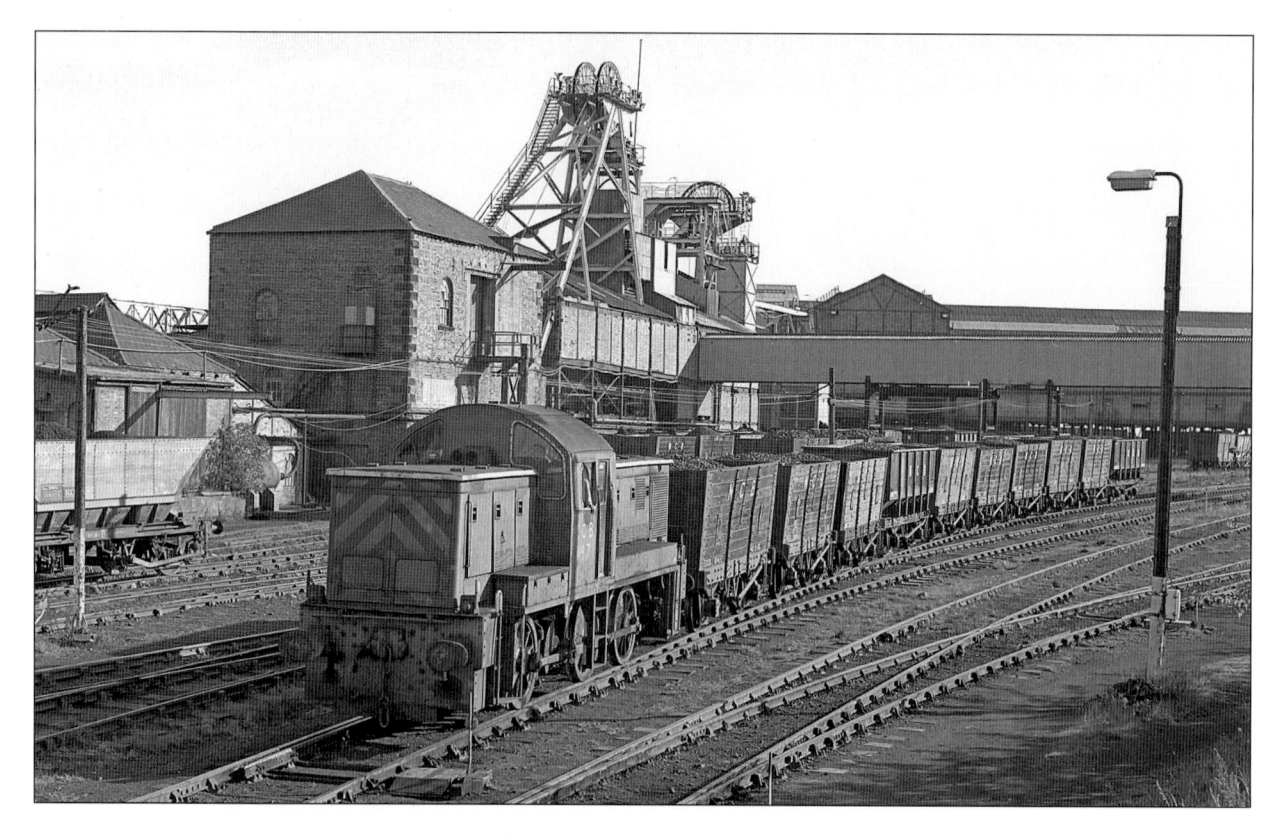

ABOVE: NCB No. 7 (former BR No. D9518) is the Paxman here shunting a rake of internal "fulls" at Ashington Colliery on Saturday 5th October 1985. *Neville Stead*

BELOW: With the end of NCB operations on the Ashington Colliery Railway looming, hundreds of internal wagons were gathered up and placed in store at New Moor to await scrapping. This was the scene looking towards Linton in 1986. The new order is apparent with Butterwell opencast and its loading bunker visible in the left distance and the line from it to Ashington with modernised level crossing threading between the wagons. This line would still be used but only by BR trains. *Adrian Booth*

ABOVE: The building dominating this picture was the nerve centre of the Ashington Railway, being both signal box and operations control. This somewhat bleak scene recorded on Tuesday 17th February 1987 with the end of internal NCB operations only weeks away shows Paxmans and other diesel locos lined up with little or no work to do while the sidings on the right are empty. Yet as late as 1980, 14 loco shifts were required, ten to cover two daytime shifts and four at night. During the day, one worked the colliery mainly weighing and stabling full wagons, one handled incoming coal for washing and shunted Duke Street landsale yard, one worked to and from Lynemouth, one to and from New Moor, and one assisted as required. Besides these, two more were outstationed at Lynemouth.

BELOW: It's all over for the Ashington Railway and the NCB has hired a Class 08 from BR to do what work remains. No. 08888 is seen shunting redundant internal wagons at New Moor alongside the somewhat dilapidated Ashington Loop signal cabin on Friday 20th March 1987, just a week before the end of NCB rail operations. *Both Neville Stead*

ABOVE: Back in happier times, Robert Stephenson & Hawthorns 0-6-0T No. 39 passes Woodhorn Colliery while working a Stephenson Locomotive Society/Manchester Locomotive Society railtour along the NCB line from Lynemouth to Ashington. Coal winding ceased at Woodhorn in 1971 and by the 1980s the separate NCB line from Ashington to Woodhorn had been abandoned and replaced by a connection with BR at Hirst. Now a museum, Woodhorn is all that remains of Northumberland's once huge coal industry. *N. Stead colln.*

BELOW: Literally the end of the line. This British Rail photo shows the sidings at Lynemouth in 1989(or Ellington South Coal Preparation Plant to give its official name since 1983) with loaded Cawoods containers awaiting dispatch to Ellesmere Port for shipping to Ireland. The British Coal locomotive is Andrew Barclay 0-6-0 diesel hydraulic 584 of 1973, rebuilt in 1987 and again in 1990, its final works number being Hunslet Barclay 6917.